The Adirondack.

Burt.

THE ADIRONDACK.

THE ADIRONDACK;

OR

Life in the Woods.

BY

J. T. HEADLEY,
AUTHOR OF "WASHINGTON AND HIS GENERALS," ETC.

NEW YORK:
BAKER AND SCRIBNER,
145 NASSAU STREET AND 36 PARK ROW.
1853.

C. W. BENEDICT, *Stereotyper,*
201 *William street, cor. of Frankfort*

LIST OF PLATES.

H. J. RAYMOND, ESQ

MY DEAR RAYMOND:

THOUGH you failed to accompany me in my trip to the Adirondack Region, yet I often thought of you in my long marches and lonely bivouacks. Filling at that time a large place in my memory, and always a much larger one in my heart, permit me to inscribe these letters to you as a token of my regard and esteem.

Very sincerely and truly yours,

J. T. HEADLEY.

NEW YORK, March 31, 1849.

CONTENTS.

CONTENTS.

CONTENTS.

CONTENTS.

XXVIII.

XXIX.

XXX.

XXXI.

XXXII.

PREFACE.

THE letters in this volume embrace two different summers which I spent in the forest. An attack on the brain first drove me from the haunts of men to seek mental repose and physical strength in the woods. The decision of an able physician, which was that I "must go where a printed page could not meet my eye, and I should be forced to take constant exercise in the open air, or ——————" impelled me to undertake at first what two years after I prosecuted with pleasure.

Thus much for the *reasons* which first induced me to penetrate the pathless and unknown wilderness of central New York.

I *publish* the results of my two trips, because I wish to make that portion of our State better known; for it bears the same relation to us that the Highlands do to Scotland, and the Oberland to Switzerland. That relation will be acknowledged yet, and every summer will witness throngs of travelers on their way to those wild mountains, and surpassingly beautiful lakes. No such scenery is to be found in our picturesque country, and none, that in my opinion, will match it this side of the Alps. Descriptions cannot, of course, give an adequate idea of it, as Prof. Emmons, in his work embraced in the great Geological Report of the State says:

"It is not, however, by description that the scenery of this region can be made to pass before the eye of the imagination; it must be witnessed, the solitary summits in the distance, the cedars and firs which clothe the rocks and shores must be seen; the solitude must be felt or if it is broken by the scream of the panther, the shrill cry of the northern diver, or the shout of the hunter; the echo from the thousand hills must be heard before all the truth in the scene can be realized."

After such a glowing description emboded in our *State Reports*, I think there is little danger that anything I shall say will be considered as exaggerated.

Some may object to the want of gravity, or as others will term it, "dignity," in these letters. All that I can say, is, they are a faithful transcript of my feelings and experience, and hence the fault if it be one, has no remedy but in dishonesty.

In the woods, the mask that society compels one to wear

is cast aside, and the restraints which the thousand eyes and reckless tongues about him fasten on the heart, are thrown off, and the soul rejoices in its liberty and again becomes a child in action. The ludicrous incident, the careless joke, the thrilling story, the eager chase, are all in place in the forest, and as harmless as the sports of the deer.

I hate hypocrisy in an author—writing not as he feels but as he knows bigoted or narrow-minded men think he *ought* to feel—moralizing on paper where he never thought of it in fact, and giving us theological disquisitions on doctrinal points

"When the bosom is full and the thoughts are high,"

with the floods of excitement and rapture which some wondrous and glorious spectacle has awakened. Nature and the Bible are in harmony—they both speak one language to the heart—yet in the wilderness there is no formality in the expression of one's feelings. A man

"Laughs when he's merry,
And sighs when he's sad,"

without thinking or caring how it would appear in the saloon or grave assemblage.

The engravings are from original drawings by the distinguished artists Messrs. Ingham, Durand, Gignoux, and

Hill of Vermont to whom I feel deeply indebted for their kindness. These give a value to the work I could not otherwise claim for it.

I am sorry that I could get no sketches of some of the romantic and beautiful scenery of the more central regions but no artist has ever yet ventured into them. At some future day there will be a collection of those views made, which will not be surpassed in beauty by any in Europe.

The Moose Lakes described in one of the letters, I have never seen, but a friend of mine, who has once been through the wilderness with me, furnished the material, and for the sake of uniformity, I used it as my own.

GENERAL DESCRIPTION OF THE COUNTRY.

To give the reader some idea of the central portion of New York, in which the scenes of this work are laid, and through which I traveled; and that he may not regard it mere child's play to penetrate it, I would say that across it either way is about the distance from New York to Albany—varying from a hundred to a hundred and fifty miles. It is the same as if the whole country from New York to Albany, and extending, also, fifty miles each side of the Hudson, was an unbroken wilderness, crossed by no road, enlivened by no cultivation, not a keel disturbing its waters, while bears, panthers, wolves, moose and deer were the only lords of the soil.

Imagine such a tract of country, about the size of Massachusetts and Connecticut put together, most of which lies a neglected waste, through which you must make your way with the compass, sustained by what your own skill can secure, and you will obtain a faint conception of the Adirondack region. And yet, you will hardly get a correct one, because there would not enter into it the gloomy gorges and savage mountains that everywhere roll it into disorder. I shall furnish, however, the best description, by giving an extract from a letter of Professor Farrand N. Benedict, of Vermont University, whose able report in the Geological Work of our State, and reports, also, to the Senate, on the capabilities of this section for slack water navigation, have been of equal service to science and to the practical man.

In a letter to me, which the reader will acknowledge to be written with singular clearness and beauty, he says:

"The northern section of New York, embracing the county of Hamilton, and the most of the counties of Essex, Clinton, Franklin, St. Lawrence, Herkimer, Lewis, Warren, and Fulton, has hitherto resisted the march of improvement, and still remains, with a few solitary exceptions, an unsubdued forest. Until recently, little has been known of its physical resources, and of its adaptedness to the wants of man in his civilized state. Regarded as an unproductive waste, it has left the vague and transient impression on the mind that it answered well enough, the only purpose of its existence, to constitute a barrier between the Mohawk and St. Lawrence Rivers, and to prevent the waters of Lake Ontario from carrying desolation with them into the valley of Champlain. It seems until lately to have failed to awaken that interest in its behalf, tc which it is 'ustly en titled, in view of the recent developments of its mineral, and even of its agricultural capabilities.

This section of country, which is frequently denominated the Plateau of Northern New York, is washed at its western base by the Black River and Lake Ontario—at its northwestern by the St. Lawrence—at its eastern by Lake Champlain—and at its southern by the Mohawk River. Settlements and civilization have advanced from five to twenty-five miles up the valleys and slopes of this elevated table, where they are met by the nearly uninterrupted wilderness of the interior. The *general* surface of this region as indicated by the lakes and streams, and in many instances, especially in the western part, of the extensive valleys which they drain, is nearly a horizontal plane, with a medium elevation above tide of 1700 feet. This elevated surface is attained by a rapid ascent from its base, in a distance of some ten or twenty miles, except where the grade is occasionally reduced, and the distance proportionably increased by valleys and streams. The slope is the most rapid from the Black River and Lake Champlain, declining more gently to the Mohawk, and still more so towards the St. Lawrence and the low country of Canada.

"This table is divided transversely into two nearly equal portions by a broad valley of variable width, which meets the shores of Lake Champlain at Plattsburgh. The valley extends in a southwesterly direction up the Saranac River to the beautiful cluster of lakes of that name—thence with no intervening ridge it passes up the Raquette River, through Long and Raquette Lakes; and thence in the same general direction, and with no opposing barrier, down the Moose River and its chain of picturesque lakes, and terminates in Oneida County, near Boonville. This valley is remarkable for its extent—being about 150 miles in length—for its nearly uniform direction, although it is formed by the basins of three different systems of waters—for the productiveness of its soil in the upper sections of its course—and especially for its almost unparalleled line of natural navigation.

"The western portion of the table, or rather that which is situated west of this valley, presents a varied and picturesque, though not a mountainous surface. The Adirondack Mountains are seen towards the east, with their bare and rocky summit, dim in the distance, projecting their spurs clothed with black forests to the shores of this central line of waters. Proceeding westwardly from this line, the physical aspect of the country undergoes a marked and immediate change. The mountains are reduced to *hills* of moderate elevations; and, instead of being covered with rugged and sterile peaks, their rounded summits display a luxuriant growth of valuable timber. They appear to be disposed without much conformity to any general system of arrangement. They are frequently solitary, and whenever they can aggregate in groups or clusters, their positions are determined by the local arrangements of the neighboring waters. Between the lakes, or rather ponds, of this uniform section, which are disseminated in singular precision over the whole plateau, the surface rises gently from the shores into swells of arable land, excepting the southern declivities which are often abrupt and precipitous.

The eastern part of the plateau, embracing a tract of country about 50 miles wide and 140 miles in length, and terminated by the Raquette Valley on the west, is decidedly Alpine in its physical aspect. Its apparently confused wilderness of mountains is found, on close examination, to be disposed in ranges nearly parallel to the valley above mentioned. These terminate in successive bold and rocky promontories on the western shore of Lake Champlain. The chains increase in elevation as they approach the interior, until they attain their greatest altitude and grandeur in the most western one of the series. This has a northern termination at Trembleau Point, and thrusts its southern extremity into the bed of the Mohawk at Little Falls. It consists of an extended aggregation of mountain masses, resting on bases that are elevated nearly 2000 feet above tide. Many of these throw their bare and pointed summits of rock to the perpendicular altitude of about a mile above the surface of the ocean. The vastness of their elevations, the almost endless variety of their forms, their confused and disorderly arrangement, and the deep forests that are interrupted only by the lakes at their bases and the rocks and snows of their summits, invest the eastern half of the table with unrivalled solitude and sublimity."

This vast mountain chain rises and sinks along the horizon in such colossal proportions that one imagines himself in the Alps. The highest peak of the Catskill is only three thousand and some hundred feet in height, yet here are summits rising out of the bosom of forests nearly twice its altitude. Mount Tahawus is over a mile high, while Whiteface, Nipple Top, Mount Seward, Santenoni, Dix's Peak, Mount McMartin and Mount McIntyre, rise each five thousand feet into the heavens. Shall I mention Owl's Head, Mount Emmons, Schroon Mountains, North River and Boreas Mountains, three thousand feet high; or Bald Peak and Raven Hill, and a host of others two thousand feet and upwards? Why, the Catskill range, majestic as it is, is a dwarf beside these gigantic mountains. From the top of one of them, you see for nearly four hundred miles in circumference. To wander among them is the hardest toil that a forest life presents. Without roads, your only reliance the guide and compass, you are compelled to wade streams, cross marshes, and climb over vast tracts of fallen timber, and at last, when night comes on, pull your own couch from the fir trees around. If it were not that a chain of lakes extends the entire length of this wilderness, cutting it in two, it would be impenetrable. Along these sheets of water—from one to another, and around rapids and cataracts, the adventurer rows his boat or carries it on his head. I have made this statement that one may see at the outset to what kind of a region I wish to introduce him.

I.

UP THE HUDSON—IN THE WOODS—TROUT FISHING—A QUEER FISH.

Backwoods, June 23.

Dear H——:

The steam is up—the pipes are spitting forth in furious disgust volumes of vapor—the last bell is ringing, and amid the clatter of carriages, the shouts of men and clouds of steam, we are off to the centre of the Hudson, and, stretching away, like a gallant steed, rapidly divide the water northward.

As I stand on the deck and think of the broad, deep forest and its rushing streams, a feeling of freedom steals over me, I have been a stranger to, for months. The chains of conventional life begin to fall off, link after link, and I fancy I feel my blood take a new spring already. This chasing after health, though, is a discouraging business. To spend half of one's life in keeping the other half from going out, is not, I am convinced, the chief end of man—still, it must sometimes be done, and then the pathless woods, the long and steady stretch up the mountain side and the coarse fare, are better than all the "poppies and mandrigoras" of the world to "medicine" not only the body but the mind. Your Saratoga water and Nahant bathing and Rockaway dinner tables will do, perhaps, for healthy men, cripples and women. But for the reduced system that needs tone and manliness given it, strong physical exercise is demanded.

I passed through Saratoga Springs without stopping even to dine, but compensated for the neglect over some trout at Glen's Falls. Arriving at Lake George just before sunset, I engaged a man to carry me on, some twenty miles farther that evening. We halted a few moments at twilight at a lonely tavern on an elevated ridge, made still more desolate by the self murder of the proprietor, the year before, over whose grave a whip-poor-will was pouring its shrill and rapid note. Soon after, we began to enter the Spruce Mountain, where, for miles, not even a hut appears to cheer the sight. In the meantime, the sky became overcast, and night came down black and threatening. The darkness at length grew so impenetrable that we could not see the horses, nor even the wagon in which we rode. Up long hills, and down into deep gulfs, with the invisible branches sweeping our faces at almost every step, we traveled on, seeing nothing but utter blackness, and not knowing but the next moment we should stumble over a precipice, or be tumbled down the slope of a "dugway." My driver, in the meantime, got excessively nervous—he had never traveled the road before, and this feeling his way, or rather allowing his horses to feel it without venturing the least control over their movements, seemed to him not the safest mode of procedure, and so after muttering awhile to himself various rather forcible expressions, he stopped and got out. Going to the heads of the horses he commenced leading them. I supposed at first that something was the matter with the harness, and said nothing; but soon finding myself moving on in the darkness, I called out to know what he was doing. "I'm afraid," he replied, "to ride, it is so dark, and I'm going to lead my horses." Just then, there came a bright flash of lightning, revealing the still and boundless forest on every side, and throwing into momentary, but bold relief, shivered trunks and blackened stumps, and last though not least important, the horses, with my driver at their head. An instantaneous and utter blackness followed—falling on everything like a mighty pall—and then came the sullen thunder, swelling gradually from the low growl into the deep vibrating peal that shook the hills. It was my turn to feel nervous now, and the idea of walking out a thunder-storm at midnight, in these mountains, was not to be entertained a moment. Unfortunately, I can bear the worst fate better than suspense; so calling out in a tone not to be mistaken, I said, "come, get in and drive on, and drive fast, too—if we break down, we will bivouack the rest of the night under the wagon, but as for going at this snail's pace, and a thunder storm gathering over our heads, I will not permit it." With a grunt at my rashness, he clambered in and started on. "Come," said I, "whip up, neck or nothing, I can't stand this." Getting into a smart trot, we passed rapidly along, expecting every moment to feel the shock that should stop us for the night, or find ourselves describing the arc of a circle, down some declivity, the bottom of which, we could only speculate upon. Ever and anon came the sudden lightning, rending the gloom, succeeded by the rolling, rattling thunder-peal, that made the horses jump, not to mention our own pulsations. Brushed every few steps by an overhanging branch, as if struck by a mysterious hand, we kept resolutely on—the good horses picking their way like Alpine mules, and the road proving itself to be far better than our fears.

At length, just as the heavy drops began to fall, we emerged into a little valley, in which nestled a rude village, the meadows of which seemed to be one mass of phosphorescence. The fire flies hung in countless numbers over the surface, forming almost a solid body of light. The effect was indescribable; all around was Egyptian darkness, except that single level spot on which the incessant flashes made a constant, yet ever tremulous light. At first, it seemed an illusion, so fluctuating and confused did everything appear; but as the eye, aided by the judgment, got accustomed to the scene, it became a beautiful creation, made on purpose to cheer the night and lessen the gloom that overhung the world.

Ah! how delicious it is after such a ride to stand under a roof and hear the big drops dashing against the windows and sides of the house, and the thunder pealing harmlessly without; you laugh at the elements which you had feared, and feel as if you had baffled an enemy whose ravings now were impotent and foolish. The rudest room is then pleasant, and the hardest bed soft as down. A delightful calm succeeds the turbulence of feeling, and you are at peace with all the world.

I will not weary you with an account of my next morning's ride, nor of the thorough drenching I received.

Arriving at a clearing, I had hardly swallowed some dinner before I donned my India-rubber leggings and plunged into a splendid stream near by, after trout. The very first cast I made, I took one, and kept taking them, till, at the end of two hours, I had fifty fine fellows. The best one of all, however, I lost. I had approached with great caution a noble pool, made by a rapid current that shot along a ledge of rocks, then spread out into an open basin. Seating myself carefully on a narrow shelf, I threw my fly, and moving it slowly in an oblique direction across the stream, soon saw a great fellow rise to the surface In a twinkling, he was hooked; but just at that moment I heard a tremendous splashing in the water above me, accompanied by something halfway between a grunt and a groan. I was startled, and turning my eyes in the direction of the tumult, saw my companion floundering in the water. With a short crooked pole, he had been endeavoring to mount a smooth, slippery rock and cast his cord-line into a hole where it looked as if trout might lurk. Just as he was fetching back his rod with a tremendous swing, his foot slipped and over he rolled into the swift current, making the splashing that had startled me so. His hat was off and his long hair streamed over his face, as now up and now down he struggled to steady his uncertain footing. At length, he brought up against a rock, and "thunder and lightning," were the first words that escaped his lips, as he looked around to determine his whereabouts. He was a capital subject for a picture, as he thus stood, bareheaded, hanging on the rock, and muttering to himself. Between the fright and the laugh, I lost my trout, but I have made my mark on him and will have him yet

II.

DANDY TURNED FARMER—TROUT FISHING, &c—CHRISTENING A BARN.

BACKWOODS, June 28.

DEAR H——:

THERE is not a wilder region in our country than the northern parts of Warren and Hamilton Counties. An almost unbroken wilderness stretches away from the Adirondack Mountains, from a hundred to a hundred and fifty miles across. Imagine such a wilderness in the heart of New York State, in which you may wander month after month without stumbling on a clearing. There are places in it never yet trod by the foot of a white man. It is not merely an uncultivated country, but a succession of ragged mountains, darkened with pine and hemlock—ploughed up with ravines and rendered barren by rocks and swamps. An over-wrought brain has driven me into these solitudes for rest and quiet—my only companions being my rifle and fishing rod. We talk in New York of going into the "*country*." But let Saratoga be exchanged for "Long Lake," Nahant for "Indian Lake," and New Rochelle for the gloomy shore of Jesup's River, and our fashionables would get an entirely different idea of the "*country*." True, it is lonely at first—after being accustomed to the din and struggle of Broadway and Wall street to sit as I now do, with a wide forest, climbing the steep mountains, to bound my vision, and the little clearing around me black with stumps, coming up even to the door of the log house. All day long, and not the sound of a single wheel, but in the place of it the cawing of crows, the scream of the woodpecker, and the roar of a torrent dashing over the rocks in the sullen forest below. The very stumps have a forlorn look, and it seems a complete waste of time and music for the birds to sing, having no one to listen to them. It must be they do it to hear the echo of their own voices, which these wild woods send back with incredible distinctness and sweetness. But if one is not entirely spoiled, he soon attunes himself to the harmony of nature, and a new life is born within him. To most of us, life has—as the Germans would say, an "Einseitigkeit," (a one-

sidedness). The "Fielseitgkeit," (the many-sidedness) few experience. Ah, it is this "Einseitigkeit," that renders all reform so difficult; and bigotry and prejudice so irresistible. Men must *experience* the "Fielseitgkeit," to know it, but circumstances chain them to the "one-sided" view, and so we go stumbling on in the old paths, or like an old mill horse round and round in the same circle, stereotyping anew the groans and complaints of our fathers. Here a man will toil for forty years and die poor, while in the city a successful speculation often ensures a life of idleness and luxury. Industry then is *not* always the sure road to wealth.

But I will not weary you with an essay on social life, I will only say that it is a poor argument which meets our complaints, from the pulpit and press, viz., "After all, happiness is about equally divided." This maxim is believed, because it is the converse of a true proposition, which is, "one man is about as miserable as another." That is, the laws of Nature and Heaven are such that he who accumulates to live a life of idleness is made as miserable as the man he impoverishes in order to do it. Thus, it is true, that happiness is pretty equally divided, because the misery the present covetous, grasping spirit works *is* pretty equally divided.

These thoughts work in me here in the woods as I lean on my rifle, and look on that sturdy backwoodsman making the forest ring with his axe as he devotes himself to a life of toil and ignorance. Ah, our religion but half performs its work. It simply turns the *wild animal* into a *domestic* one, but leaves him an *animal* still. It does not elevate him, so that the poor can be intelligent, refined, and spiritual. He is still doomed to toil, toil, for the mere *animal nature.* Religion was designed by its great Author to accomplish more than this.

My stopping place is at the house of an old friend, on the frontier of this wild region, who, when I last knew him, was called a New York dandy. Designed by his friends for a profession, he broke away from his studies and entered upon a mercantile life. In the crash of 1837, he went down with the multitude. Land, scattered here and there over the country, was all that was left him to fall back upon, and he resolved to turn farmer. I could hardly believe my eyes, when I saw what a rock and mountain farm he was on. As I came up to the door, he was engaged in filling a *straw bed for his baby*—queer occupation this, for a *ci-devant* dandy. The next morning as he drove off to the woods with his oxen, one would never have dreamed he had once sauntered up and down Broadway. His wife, a refined and intelligent woman, at first sunk under this change, but rallying her good sense, she has adapted herself to her situation, and now makes butter, &c., like a good house-wife. My friend seemed happy, but I thought it must be assumed, and so I asked him how this compared with New York. "I am happier here," he replied, "I prefer this life to that of the city." The delicate young merchant is spreading into the broad-shouldered working man. I confess I admired him, and the second day I told him I would help him work, if on the succeeding one he would play with me. He agreed to this arrangement, and so I doffed my coat and went into the field with him, My appetite for the plain dinner was a trifle beyond what is termed good, and my slumbers that night deep as oblivion.

The next morning I claimed the fulfillment of his promise, and he shouldered his long limber ash pole which he had cut from the forest, and peeled to make it lighter, and we entered the dark hemlock forest that overhangs the "trout-brook," and were soon in the midst of rare sport. By the way, pay no regard to the list of fancy flies which sportsmen often make so much ado about. The *red and black hackles* are the best for our latitude *all* seasons of the year. With this short episode, follow me in fancy, down the stream, packing the bright spotted trout away into my basket, until we come to a dark overhanging precipice. Here the stream flows in a broad sheet against and under the mountain, and disappears from sight to appear again farther on. This precipice, shooting at an angle of 45 degrees over the current, turning it back on itself, and forcing it downward, forms a deep, black pool, covered with the foam-bubbles which circle and dart like live creatures in the eddies. There, on the very edge of the eddy, I have cast my fly. It has hardly moved before, look! what a noble fellow makes the water foam as he throws an arch into the air, his white belly gleaming like a silver arrow as he goes. Snap goes the line, and he vanishes. Ah, he was a fat one, and that last fling of his by which he cleared himself, made every nerve in me tingle.

But I will have his mate. Quickly noosing another snell, I drag again the deep pool, and there the other shoots—the beauty, and I have him; I cannot play him—the bushes and flood-wood and rocks, are too thick,—and he flounders like a sturgeon—I must lift him or lose him. My slender rod almost doubles, and quivers with the load; but the good stick holds, and the fellow is landed. There is absolutely terror in his great black eye as he lies and pants on the rock. I can't help it, my speckled beauty, it's a world where we prey on each other. Beside, I have had nothing but fried pork for three days, and I already gloat in imagination over your salmon-colored flesh. I have gone but half a mile, and let us see, I have *forty*. That will do for to-day, and we will turn home.

Passing through a clearing on a side-hill, on our way back, we came upon a *barn raising*, called here a "bee," because all the neighbors are invited to assist. The rough frame was up, and a man was sitting on the ridge pole, hallooing, "Here's a frame without a name, and what'll ye call it? Here's a frame without a name, and what'll ye call it? Here's a frame without a name, and what'll ye call it?"—"*Side-hill drag*," was shouted back from the sturdy group below. It was christened with a hurra, and up went two old drag-frames to the plates where they were left dangling in the air. I could not but smile at this curious christening, yet the man was as proud of his wit, as the politician of his toast on some great festive occasion, and had as good reason to be for aught I know

Yours truly,

III.

"DRIVING TREES"—BENIGHTED IN THE WOODS.

INDIAN LAKE, June 30.

DEAR H——:

DID you ever fall a tree? If not, the experiment is worth your while—for the consciousness of power it awakens, and the absolute terror it inspires, as the noble and towering fabric at length yields to your assaults, amply repay the labor. The first stroke into the huge trunk sends a slight shiver through all the green top; but as stroke follows stroke, the old king of the woods seems to despise your puny efforts, and receives the blows in silent contempt. But as fibre after fibre is severed, and the heart is at last reached and pierced, a groan passes up through the lofty stem. Then comes a cracking, as if the very seat of life was broken up, and the frightened thing sways and staggers a moment, as if to steady its enormous bulk, then bows its tall head in submission, and without another effort, and with a shock that shakes the hills around, falls to the ground. There he lies with all his great arms crushed under him, stretched a lifeless corse along the earth. His brethren nod and tremble a moment above him, as if they felt the overthrow, then all is still again. Thus the other day I brought a brave old hemlock to the ground, and when I saw the lofty green mass first begin to sway, and then heard the snapping and rending of the tough fibres of the trunk, a feeling of terror stole over me. This a backwoodsman would doubtless call transcendentalism, if he knew the meaning of the term, but there is no transcendentalism in swinging a heavy axe for an hour to fetch one of these sturdy trees down.

But felling a single tree is a small matter compared to a process called here "*driving trees*"? Don't imagine a whole "Birnam" forest on the move "for Dunsinane," like a flock of sheep going to market; but sit down with me here on the side-hill, and look at that opposite mountain slope. Just above that black fallow, or as they call it here "foller," there, in that deep grove, five as good choppers as ever swung an axe, have made the woods ring for the last three hours with their steady strokes, and yet not a tree has fallen. But, look! now one begins to bend—and hark, crack! crack! crash! crash! a whole forest seems falling, and a gap is made like the path of a whirlwind. Those choppers worked both down and up the hill, cutting each tree half in two, until they got twenty or more thus partially severed. They did not cut at random, but chose each tree with reference to another. At length a sufficient number being prepared, they felled one that was certain to strike a second that was half-severed, and this a third, and so on, till fifteen or twenty came at once with that tremendous crash to the ground. Here is labor-saving without machinery. The process is called "*driving trees*," and it is driving them with a vengeance.

A day or two since I made an engagement with an Indian to go out at night, deer hunting. We were sure, he said, of taking one. Having nothing in the meanwhile to do, and the pure air and bright sky tempting a stroll in the solemn woods, I shouldered my rifle and started off. After proceeding about a mile, thinking of anything but game, I was suddenly aroused from my reverie by the spring of a deer just ahead. I looked up, and there, with an arching neck and waving tail, stood a beautiful doe. Quick as thought she darted away, but when she had gone about 25 or 30 rods stopped again. At first I could not see her, for she had halted behind a clump of bushes; but at length I observed a reddish spot, about the size of the crown of my cap, between the leaves. I hesitated to shoot, for I knew it was the broadside, and one of my small bullets (my rifle carries 83 to the pound) planted there, might not fetch her down till she had run ten miles. However, it was my only chance, so I took a steady aim, and fired. A wild spring into the open forest told me she was hit, and as she leaped madly away, the tail she carried a moment before like a plume, was hugged close to her legs. Hence I was not surprised when I came to where she had stood, to find large drops of blood on the leaves. I took the trail and followed on. It was slow work, without a dog, and how far I went I know not, but I did not give it up till the increasing darkness blotted the traces from my sight. I then turned to go back, but, alas, had not the slightest idea of the course I had traveled; and the sun being now down, and the high trees blotting out everything but a little space of sky overhead, I was utterly at a loss which way to go. I pushed on, however, trusting more to luck than my own knowledge or sagacity. But night having at length come down in earnest, every step was taken at random. Heavy and disheartened, I sat down on a log, and (thanks to my Alpine match-box,) soon struck a light. It was 9 o'clock. Well, thinks I to myself, it's only a little over six hours to daylight, and I may as well stop and wait as to be knocking my head against these trees without getting any nearer home, nay, perhaps, farther off. Looking around, I espied a knoll with a rock on it. Here, kindling a fire to keep off the musquitoes and black flies that were devouring me at a rate that would soon leave nothing for the wolves to lunch on, I sat down and waited for the leaden hours to wear away. It seems a very trifling thing when we read about it, to pass a night in the woods, especially when you know that the beasts of prey which roam the forest, dare not attack you—it *is* a trifling thing to a backwoodsman, but just try it yourself once. I do not affirm that you will be frightened; but as Lugarto was accustomed to say, you will "*be nervous.*" It was warm, and there was no danger; neither was I lost, for I knew a walk of an hour or two in the morning would bring me out yet I could not sleep. Bryant says in his Thanatopsis, that it should be a great comfort to a man in death, to know that he "lies down with kings and the powerful of the earth." I don't know how it may affect one "*in death*," but I *do* know that in vigorous health, it requires more than the mere reflection that the "kings and the great ones of the earth" are snoozing on their couches of down, to make one sleep sweetly in the solemn woods without a friend near him. If I felt inclined to doze, the snapping of the fire, or the stealthy tread of a fox or hedgehog, would startle me from my disturbed slumbers—and there stood the tall trees in the fire light, their huge trunks fading away in the gloom like the columns of some old cathedral at twilight. Once, I could have sworn I saw a bear, and was on the point of shooting, but finally concluded to take a fire-brand in one hand and my rifle in the other, and go towards it, when lo! it turned out to be a *black stump*. I let it sleep on, and went back to my fire, determined to have a nap. It was all in vain, and yet I had slept soundly in places where I felt at the time there was infinitely more danger than here. I had slept lashed to a bench when the storm was springing our masts, and the sea falling in thunder on the deck of our staggering ship—I had slept amid the "Alps and Appenines," nay, worse, in the cabriolet of a French diligence, beside the yelling *conducteur.* I had slept on the hard floor, and beside living and dead men, but I could not sleep *here.* There was something so awfully solemn and mysterious in that mighty forest—in the rustle of the night breeze through the tops of the hemlocks, and the flutter now and then of a bird disturbed on its perch, that my heart beat audibly in my bosom. Just as my nervousness began to be particularly annoying, there came a flash of lightning, followed by the low growl of distant thunder. This was something I had not calculated upon, and I said to myself, "Well, there is a prospect of my trying Preissnitz's system now, for there will be cold bathing in plenty before morning, and my diet is spare enough, heaven knows, for I haven't even a red-squirrel to roast for my supper. I shall be thankful if one of these rotten hemlocks does not have the rubbing of me down after my bath." Just then the blast swept through the forest like the roar of the sea, and all was still again. Another flash, and as I live, there stood a man amid the trees; I waited in breathless suspense for a second flash but the tread of feet prevented the necessity, and the next instant the Indian (a civilized one) whom I had engaged to go deer hunting with me, approached. The amount of affection I at that moment entertained for the red-skinned gentleman, would, I think, satisfy my wife, if I am ever fortunate enough to have one. He had seen the light of my fire above the trees, and supposing I was lost came after me; and I assure you it was the most profitable *short journey* he ever made. It turned out that I was not two miles from the settler's house from which I had started. We reached it about 2 o'clock, and I slept on my straw bed that night without thinking of "the great ones of the earth"

Yours truly

IV.

A RIVER IN THE FOREST—LIFE—"DRIVING THE RIVER."

BACKWOODS, June 6.

DEAR H——:

DID you ever witness a log driving? It is one of the curiosities of the backwoods, where streams are made to subserve the purpose of teams. On the steep mountain side, and along the shores of the brook which in spring time becomes a fiery torrent, tearing madly through the forest, the tall pines and hemlocks are felled in winter and dragged or rolled to the brink. Here every man marks his own, as he would his sheep, and then rolls them in, when the current is swollen by the rains. The melted snow along the acclivities comes in an unbroken sheet of water down, and the streams rise as if by magic to the tops of their banks, and a broad, resistless current goes sweeping like a live and gloomy thing through the deep forest.

The foam bubbles sparkle on the dark bosom that floats them on, and past the boughs that bend with the stream, and by the precipices that frown sternly down upon the tumult; while the rapid waters shoot onward like an arrow, or rather a visible spirit on some mysterious errand, seeking the loneliest and most fearful passages the untrodden wild can furnish. I have seen the waves running like mad creatures in mid ocean, and watched with strange feelings the moonlit deep as it gently rose and fell like a human bosom in the still night; but there is something more mysterious and fearful than these in the calm yet lightning-like speed of a deep, dark river, rushing all alone in its might and majesty through the heart of a vast forest. You cannot see it till you stand on the brink, and then it seems utterly regardless of you or the whole world without, hasting sternly forward to the accomplishment of some dread purpose.

But such romance as this never enters the heart of your backwoodsman. The first question he puts himself, as he thrusts his head through the branches and looks up and down the channel, is—"Is the stream high enough to run logs?" If so, then fall to work: away go the logs, one after another, down the mountain, and down the bank, with a bound and a groan, and splash into the water.

The heavy rains about the first of July, had so swollen the stream near which I am *located*, that all thoughts of fishing for several days were abandoned, and the log drivers had it entirely to themselves. So, strolling through the forest, I soon heard the continuous roar that rose up through the leafy solitudes, and in a few moments stood on a shelving rock, and saw the dark, swift stream before me, as it issued from the cavernous green foliage above, and disappeared without a struggle in the same green abyss below. I stood for a long time lost in thought. How much like life was that current in its breathless haste—how like it, too, in its mysterious appearance and departure! It shot on my sight without a token of its birthplace, and vanished without leaving a sign whither it had gone. So comes and goes this mysterious life of ours—this fearful time-stream, sweeping so noiselessly and steadily forward. And there, where that bubble dances and swims, now floating calmly though swiftly along the surface, and now caught in an eddy, and whirled in endless gyrations round, and now buffeted back by the hard rock against whose side it was cast, is another life symbol. Such am I, and such is every man —bubbles on the dread time-stream—one moment moving calmly over the waters of prosperity—the next, caught in the eddies of misfortune, till, bewildered and stunned, we are hurled against the rocks of discouragement. Yet, ever afloat, and ever borne rapidly on, we are moving from sight, to be swallowed up in that vast solitude, from whose echoless depths no voice has ever yet returned. Life, life, how solemn and mysterious thou art! I could weep as I lean from this rock and gaze on the dark, rushing waters—thought crowds on thought, and sad memories come sweeping up, and future forebodings mingle in the solemn gathering, and emotions no one has ever yet expressed, and feelings that have struggled since time began, for utterance, swell like that swollen water over my heart, and make me inconceivably sad here in the depths of the forest.

How long I might have stood absorbed in this half dreamy half thoughtful mood, I know not, had I not heard a shout below me. Passing down, I soon came to a steep bank, at the base of which several men were tumbling logs into the stream. I watched them for some time, and was struck with the coolness with which one would stand half under a huge embankment of logs, and hew away to loosen the whole, while another with a "handspike"* kept them back. Once, after a blow, I saw the entire mass start, when "Take care! take care!" burst in such startling tones from my lips, that the cool chopper sprung as if stung by an adder; then, with a laugh at his own foolish fright, stepped back to his place again. The man with the "handspike" never even turned his head, but with a half grunt, as much as to say "Green horn from the city," held on. It was really an exciting scene—the mad leaping away of those huge logs, and their rapid, arrowy-like movement down the stream. At length I threw off my coat, and laying my gun aside, also seized a "handspike," and was soon behind a log, tugging and lifting away. I was on the top of a high bank, and when the immense timber gave way, and bounded with a dull sound from rock to rock, till it struck with a splash into the very centre of the current, my sudden shout followed it. The first plunge took it out of sight, and when it rose to the surface again, it stood, for a single moment, perfectly still in its place, except that it rolled rapidly on its axis—the

* A wooden lever.

next moment it yielded to the impetuosity of the current and darted away as if inherent with life, and moved straight towards a precipice that frowned over the water below. Recoiling from the shock, its head swung off with the current, and away it shot out of sight.

The stream gets full of these logs, which often catch on some rock or projecting root, and accumulate till a hundred or more will be all tangled and matted together. There they lie rising and falling on the uneasy current, while a driver slowly and carefully steps from one to another, feeling with his feet and "handspike," to see where the "drag" is. When he finds it, he loosens, perhaps with a blow, the whole rolling, tumbling mass, and away it moves. Now look out, bold driver, thy footing is not of the most certain kind, and a wild and angry stream is beneath thee. Yet see how calmly he views the chaos. The least hurry or alarm and he is lost:—but no, he moves without agitation,—now balancing himself a moment, as the log he steps upon shoots downward, then quickly passing to another as that rolls under him, he is gradually working his way towards the shore. He has almost succeeded in reaching the bank, when the whole floating mass separates so far, that he can no longer step from one to another, and after looking about a moment, he quietly seats himself astraddle of one, and darts like a fierce rider down the current.

These logs are carried twenty and thirty miles in this way, passing from small streams to larger ones, through lakes and along rivers, and are finally brought up at the wished-for spot by poles across the river, which stop their further descent. Several different men club together to drive the stream, and here they pick out each one his own, by the mark he has placed upon it, as you have seen a farmer select his sheep in a pen containing several flocks.

This marking logs like sheep, was entirely new to me, and somewhat droll. I could imagine the owners at the place of rendezvous, (i. e., of the logs,) selecting them in somewhat the following manner: one cries out, "well, neighbor Jones, is that your log?" "Yes." "How do you know?" "Oh, it has my mark—*cropped on both ears and slit in the right;* and here is one belonging to you with a bob-tail, and a knot in the forehead."

This "driving the river," as it is called, is one of the chief employments of your backwoodsmen in spring time, and it is curious to see what an object of interest the river becomes. Its rise and fall are the chief topics of conversation. So goes the world—New York has its objects of interest—the country village its—and the settler on the frontier his—each one is filled with the same anxieties, hopes, fears and wishes—overcome by the same discouragements and misfortunes, and working out the same fate; man still with that mysterious soul and restless heart of his, greater than a king, and immortal as an angel, yet absorbed with straws and maddened or thrown into raptures by a little glittering dust.

V

FORESTWARD—DINNER SCENE—PREPARATIONS TO ASCEND MOUNT TAHAWUS.

BACKWOODS, July 10, 1846.

DEAR H——:

IT will be a long time before I am again by a post office where I can get a letter to you. If you wish to know the pleasure of seeing a newspaper from New York, bury yourself in the woods for three or four weeks, where not a pulsation of the great busy world can reach you, nor a word from its ten thousand tongues and pens meet your ear or eye. The sight of one, then, fresh from the press, putting in your hands again the links of that great chain of human events you had lost—re-binding you to your race, and replacing you in the mighty movement that bears all things onward, is most welcome. You cannot conceive the contrasts, nay, almost the shocks of feeling one experiences in stepping from the crowded city into the dense forest where his couch is the boughs he himself cuts, and his companions the wild deer and the birds; or in emerging again into civilized life, and listening to the strange tumult that has not ceased in his absence. One seems to have dreamed twice—nay, to be in a dream yet. Yesterday, as it were, I was walking the crowded streets of New York; last evening, in a birch-bark canoe, with an Indian beside me, nearly a day's journey from a human habitation, sailing over a lake whose green shores have never been marred by the axe of civilization, and on whose broad expanse not a boat was floating, but that which guided me and my companions on. For miles the Indian has carried this canoe on his head through the woods, and now it is breasting the waves that come rolling like fluid gold from the west. The sun is going to his repose amid the purple mountains—the blue sky seems to lift in the elastic atmosphere—the scream of the wild bird fills the solitude, and all is strange and new, while green islands untrodden by man greet us as we steer towards yonder distant point, where our camp-fire is to be lighted to-night. Glorious scene—glorious evening! with my Indian and my rifle by my side—skimming in this canoe along the clear waters, how far away seem the strifes of men and the discords of life. To-night my couch of balsam boughs shall be welcome, until the cloudless morn floods this wild scene with light.

But I find I am getting on too fast. To begin at the beginning—I started with four companions, from where I had been for some time fishing, for a stretch through the wilderness, to ascend Mount Marcy, as it is foolishly called,—properly Mount Tahawus,—and go through the famous Indian Pass. Here there are no mule paths, as in Switzerland, leading to the bases of mountains, whence you can mount to the summits; but all is woods! woods! woods! The highest and most picturesque of the Adirondack peaks lie deep in the forest, where none but an experienced guide can carry you. To reach Mount Tahawus, you must come in from Caldwell or Westport, about thirty miles, in a mail wagon, and then you have a stretch of some forty miles through the woods to the Adirondack Iron Works. There is but one road to these Works, where it stops, and he who would go farther must take to the pathless woods; indeed, it was made solely for these iron quarries, by the company which owns them

Well, here we are, in the heart of the forest, five of us, bumping along in a lumber wagon over a road you would declare a civilized team could not travel.* Now straining up a steep ascent—now whang to the axle-tree between the rocks, and now lying at an angle of forty-five degrees, and again carefully lifting ourselves over a fallen tree, we tumble and bang along at the enormous rate of two miles an hour. By dint of persuasion, the use of the whip, and a thousand "he-ups," we have acquired this velocity, and been able to keep it for the last seven hours. But man and beast grow weary—it is one o'clock, and as the forest is but half traversed, a dinner must be had in some way. In three minutes the horses are unhitched, and eating from the wagon—in three more a cheerful fire is crackling in the woods, and our knapsacks are scattered around, disgorging their contents. Here is a bit of pork, here some ham, tongue, anchovy-paste, bread, &c., &c., strung along like a column of infantry, on a moss-covered log, and each one with his pocket-knife is doing his *devoirs.* We eat with an appetite that would throw a French cook into ecstacies, did he but shut his eyes to our bill of

* It has been improved since, and is now quite good.

fare. Dinner being over, B——n, a six-footer, one of the finest specimens of a farmer and gentleman you will meet in many a day, has lighted his pipe, and is sitting on the ground with his back against a log, deep in the columns of the *Courier and Enquirer* which I received the day before we started. Young A——ld, a quiet little fellow, about eighteen years old, is stretched full length *on* the log trying to get a nap. Young S——th, tough, vigorous, and full of blood and spirits, as these old woods are of musquitoes, whose hearty laugh rings out every five minutes, as well at misfortunes as at a joke, is smoking his cigar over the *Albany Argus.* P——, one of the most careless of mortals, who is just as likely to run his head against a tree as one side of it—who, in all human probability, will have his heel on your pork before it is half toasted, or his pantaloon-strap in your tea before it is half cooled, is backed up against a tree, with his legs across a dead limb, running over the columns of the *Express.* He is one of your poetic creatures; half the time in a dream, and the other half indulging in drollery that keeps the company in a roar. He was never in the woods before, and the shadow of the mighty

Ingham. Burt.

LAKE. SANFORD

forest falls on his spirit with a strange power, awakening a world of new emotions within him. Again and again have I been startled by his "How savage! how awful!" At a little distance I myself am sitting against a stump, with the *Tribune* in my hand, telling B——n the news from Washington. This sets him going; and his sensible remarks on political subjects would make a capital leader for a paper. There you have my fellow-travelers; and you must confess there could not be better companions for a tramp of a few weeks in the forest.

Refreshed by our dinner and primitive siesta, we pushed on, and at length reached the foot of Lake Sanford, where we found Cheney cutting down trees. Embarking in his boat, we rowed slowly up to the Adirondack Iron Works. This lake is a beautiful sheet of water, without a hand-breath of cultivation upon its shores. Islands smile on you from every point, while to the right, lifts in grand composure the whole chain or rather the countless peaks of the Adirondack. Tamerack and cedar trees line the banks—in some places growing straight out over the water—the tops almost as near the surface as the roots. It seems as if they were attracted by the moisture below.

and thus grew in a horizontal direction instead of an upright one. The effect of such a strange growth along the shore, is singular in the extreme.

As we passed leisurely up the lake—now glancing away from an island—now steering along the narrow channel which separated two, we saw a white gull sitting on a solitary rock that just appeared above the water. I ascertained afterwards, that he sat there day after day, watching for fish. His nest was on the island near.

Coming near another island, Cheney rested a moment on his oars, and said, "here Mr. Ingham made a picture of the lake."

But all journeys must end, and we at length, after forcing our way up the narrow and shallow inlet, found ourselves at the Adirondack Iron Works—the loneliest place a hammer ever struck in. Forty miles to a post office or a mill—flour eight dollars a barrel, and common tea a dollar a pound in these woods, in the very heart of the Empire State! These quarries were discovered by an Indian, and made known by him to Mr. Henderson, who paid him, I believe, two shillings a day, and found him in tobacco, to take him in where the water poured over an "iron dam." From this to the top of Mount Tahawus, it is nearly twenty miles through the woods. Not a human footstep, so our guide the "mighty hunter, Cheney," tells us, has profaned it for six years, and it is two good days' work to go and return. A tramp of forty miles through a pathless forest to see one mountain, is a high price to pay, but we have resolved to do it. You must know that thirty miles in dense woods, is equal to sixty miles along a beaten track. These primeval forests are not your open groves like those south and west, through which a horse can gallop; but woven and twisted together and filled up with underbrush that prevent you from seeing ten rods ahead, and which scratch and flog you at every step, as if you were running the gauntlet.

One or two nights at least, we must sleep in the woods, and our provision be carried on our backs, and so behold us at 7 o'clock in the morning ready to start. First comes Cheney, our guide, with a heavy pack on his back filled with bread, and pork and sugar, carrying an axe in his hand with which to build our shanty and cut our fuel. Young S——th has also a pack strapped to his shoulders, while A——ld and P—— have nothing but their overcoats lashed around them;

B——n carries a tea-kettle in his hand, for he would as soon think of camping out without his pipe and tobacco, as without his tea. As for myself, I carry a green blanket tied by a rope to my shoulders, a strong hunting-knife and a large stick like the Alpine stock, which I found so great a help in climbing the Alps. Some of the worthy workmen of the furnace are looking on, doubtful whether all will hold out to the top. "Have you the pork?" says one; "Yes." "Have you the sugar and tea?" "Yes." "Have you the spy-glass?" "Yes." "Well," says Cheney, "is everything ready?" "Yes." "Then let us be off."

Yours truly.

VI.

ASCENT OF MOUNT TAHAWUS—A MAN SHOT—A HARD TRAMP—GLORIOUS PROSPECT—A CAMP SCENE.

BACKWOODS, July 12.

——— :

HURRAH! we are off, and crossing a branch of the Hudson near its source, enter the forest, Indian file, and stretch forward. It is no child's play before us; and the twenty miles we are to travel will test the blood and muscle of every one. The first few miles there is a rough path, which was cut last summer, in order to bring out the body of Mr. Henderson. It is a great help, but filled with sad associations. At length we came to the spot where twenty-five workmen watched with the body in the forest all night. It was too late to get through, and here they kindled their camp-fire, and stayed. The rough poles are still there, on which the corpse rested. "Here," says Cheney, "on this log I sat all night, and held

Mr. Henderson's little son, eleven years of age, in my arms. Oh, how he cried to be taken in to his mother; but it was impossible to find our way through the woods; and he, at length, cried himself to sleep in my arms. Oh, it was a dreadful night." A mile further on, and we came to the rock where he was shot. It stands by a little pond, and was selected by them to dine upon. Cheney was standing on the other side of the pond, with the little boy, whither he had gone to make a raft, on which to take some trout, when he heard the report of a gun, and then a scream; and looking across, saw Mr. Henderson clasp his arms twice over his breast, exclaiming, "I am shot!" The son fainted by Cheney's side; but in a few moments all stood round the dying man, who murmured, "What an accident, and in such a place!" In laying down his pistol, with the muzzle unfortunately towards him, the hammer struck the rock, and the cap exploding, the entire contents were lodged in his body. After commending his soul to his Maker, and telling his son to be a good boy, and give his love to his mother, he leaned back and died. It made us sad to gaze on the spot; and poor Cheney, as he drew a long sigh, looked the picture of sorrow.

Ingham. Burt.

Perhaps some of us would thus be carried out of the woods. He left New York as full of hope as myself; and here he met his end. Shall I be thus borne back to my friends? It is a little singular that he was always nervously afraid of fire-arms, and carried this pistol solely as a protection against wild beasts; and yet, he fell by his own hand. He never could see a man walking in the streets with a gun in his hand, without stepping to the door to inquire if it were loaded. Poor man! it was a sad place to die in; for his body had to be carried over *thirty miles* on men's shoulders, before they came to a public road.

The exhausting march, however, soon drove these sad thoughts from our minds, and we strained forward—now treading over a springy marsh—now stooping and crawling like lame iguanas, through a swamp of spruce trees, and anon following the path made by deer and moose, as they came from the mountains to the streams, or climbing around a cataract, until, at length, we reached Lake Colden, perfectly embosomed amid the gigantic mountains, and looking for all the world like an innocent child sleeping in a robber's embrace. Awfully savage and wild are the mountains that enclose this placid sheet of water. Crossing a strip of forest, we next struck the Opalescent River, so called from the opals found in its bed. The forest here is almost impassible; and so, for five miles, we kept the bed of the stream, chasing it backward to its source. The channel is one mass of rocks; and hence, our march was a constant leap from one to another, requiring a correct eye, and a steady foot, to keep the balance. Thus, zigzaging over the bed of this turbulent stream, we flitted backward and forward, like flies over the surface of a river, till, at length, I heard a shout. S——th had missed his footing, and slipping from a rock, gone plump into a deep pool. Gathering himself up, he laughed louder than the loudest, and pushed on.

Suddenly Cheney stopped and listened; for the deep bay of his hound in the distance, rang through the forest. "He has stopped something," he exclaimed; "hark, how fierce he is. I shouldn't wonder if it was a moose; for *a cow* moose, with her calf, will stop and fight a dog this time a year. If it is a moose, it would be worth while to go back." But I was after Mount Tahawus, and could ill afford to linger on the way, although soon after we heard the lowing of a moose in a distant gorge—how lonely the deep echo sounded.

At length we all came to a halt on the rocks, and prepared for dinner, and no one was more glad than myself to rest. A blazing fire was kindled of dry logs, and soon each one had his piece of fat pork on a long stick, and was holding it over the flame. I counted four pieces all coming to a focus before I added mine to the list. Putting them together was a capital arrangement, for the fat dropping off into the fire increased the blaze, and hence facilitated the cooking. Dipping my slice every few seconds into the river to freshen it, and then laying it upon my bread to preserve the gravy, I at length had the satisfaction of seeing it well done. It was eaten with an appetite that quite alarmed me, for it indicated such a radical change in my notions and taste, that I was afraid I might turn into something monstrous.

Soon after, our packs were all slung again, and we on the march. We continued diving deeper and deeper into the hills, until we at last reached the base of the mountain, and the foot of a lofty cataract. I have climbed the Alps and Appenines, but never found foot and eye in such requisition before. It was literally "right up," while the spruce trees, with their dry limbs like thorns a yard long, stuck out on every side, ready to transfix us, and compelling us to duck and dodge at every step. Now sinking through the treacherous moss that covered some gap in the rocks, and now swinging from one dead tree to another, we continued for two miles panting and straining up the steep acclivity, flogged and torn at every step. We had already gone fifteen miles, and such a winding up of the tramp was too much. H—— thought "the Millerites had better start from this elevation." A—— said 'twould "tear their ascension robes so that they would look rather shabby on the wing." T—— was sure the notion would take with them, as they

"Could make such a *dale* of the journey on *foot*."

One large athletic hunter we had taken along as an assistant, gave out, so that we were compelled frequently to halt and let him rest. The fir trees grew thicker and more dwarfish as we ascended, till they became mere shrubs, and literally matted together, so that you could not see two feet in advance of you. Through, and over these we floundered, and urged our steps; yet, tired as I was, I could not but stop and laugh to see B——n fight his way through. Rolling himself over like a cart-wheel, he would disappear in the thick evergreens—in a short time, his face, red with the fierce struggle, would rise like that of a spent swimmer's over the waves; and then, with a crash, he went out of sight again; and so kept up the battle for at least half an hour. Here we passed over the bed of a moose, which we doubtless roused from his repose, for the rank grass was still matted where he had lain. At length, we emerged upon the brow of a cliff, across a gulf at the base of which arose a bare, naked pyramid, that pushed its rocky forehead high into the heavens. This was the summit of Tahawus. A smooth grey rock, shaped like an inverted bowl, stood before us, as if on purpose to mock all our efforts. Halfway up this was S——th, looking no larger than a dog, as with his pack on his back he crawled on all fours over the rocks. Hitherto nothing could knock the fun out of him; and as he from time to time stumbled on a log, or heard the complaint of some one behind, he would sing in a comical sort of a chorus, "*go-in-up*," followed by his hearty ha-ha-ha, as if he were impervious to fatigue. To every halloo we sent after him, he would return that everlasting "*go-in-up*," sung out so funnily that we invariably echoed back his laugh, till the mountains rang again. But now he was silent—the "*go-in-up*" had become a serious matter, and it required all his breath to enable him to "go up."

As we ascended this bald cone, the chill wind swept by like a December blast; and well it might, for the snow had been gone but a few weeks. The fir trees had gradually dwindled away, till they were not taller than your finger, and now disappeared altogether; for nothing but naked rock could resist the climate of this high region. The dogs, which had hitherto scoured the forest on every side, crouched close and shivering to our side—evidently frightened, as they looked off on empty space—and all was dreary, savage, and wild.

At length we reached the top; and oh, what a view spread out before, or rather below us. Here we were more than a mile up in the heavens, on the highest point of land in the Empire State; and with one exception the highest in the Union; and in the centre of a chaos of mountains, the like of which I never saw before. It was wholly different from the Alps. There were no snow peaks and shining glaciers; but all was grey, or green, or black, as far as the vision could extend. It looked as if the Almighty had once set this vast earth rolling like the sea; and then, in the midst of its maddest flow, bid all the gigantic billows stop and congeal in their places. And there they stood, just as He froze them—grand and gloomy. There was the long swell—and there the cresting, bursting billow—and there, too, the deep, black, cavernous gulf. Far away—more than fifty miles to the south-east—a storm was raging, and the massive clouds over the distant mountains of Vermont, or rather *between* us and them, and below their summits, stood balanced in space, with their white tops towering over their black and dense bases, as if they were the margin of Jehovah's mantle folded back to let the earth beyond be seen. That far-away storm against a background of mountains, and with nothing but the most savage scenery between—how mysterious—how awful it seemed!

Mount Colden, with its terrific precipices—Mount McIntyre, with its bold, black, barren, monster-like head—White Face, with its white spot on its forehead, and countless other summits pierced the heavens in every direction. And then, such a stretch of forest, for more than three hundred miles in circumference—ridges and slopes of green, broken only by lakes that dared just to peep into view from their deep hiding-places—one vast wilderness seamed here and there by a river whose surface you could not see, but whose course you could follow by the black winding gap through the tops of the trees. Still there was beauty as well as grandeur in the scene. Lake Champlain, with its islands spread away as far as the eye could follow towards the Canadas, while the distant Green Mountains rolled their granite summits along the eastern horizon, with Burlington curtained in smoke at their feet. To the north-west gleamed out here and there the lakes of the Saranac River, and farther to the west, those along the Raquette; nearer by, Lake Sanford, Placid Lake, Lake Colden, Lake Henderson, shone in quiet beauty amid the solitude. Nearly thirty lakes in all were visible—some dark as polished jet beneath the shadow of girdling mountains; others flashing out upon the limitless landscape, like smiles to relieve the gloom of the great solitude. Through out the wide extent but three clearings were visible—all was as Nature made it. My head swam in the wondrous vision; and I seemed lifted up above the earth, and shown all its mountains and forests and lakes at once. But the impression of the whole, it is impossible to convey—nay, I am myself hardly conscious what it is. It seems as if I had seen vagueness, terror, sublimity, strength, and beauty, all embodied, so that I had a new and more definite knowledge of them. God appears to have wrought in these old mountains with His highest power, and designed to leave a symbol of His omnipotence. Man is nothing here, his very shouts die on his lips. One of our company tried to sing, but his voice fled from him into the empty space. We fired a gun, but it gave only half a report, and no echo came back, for there was nothing to check the sound in its flight. "God is great!" is the language of the heart, as it swells over such a scene.

And this is in New York, I at length exclaimed, whose surface is laced with railroads and canals, and whose rivers are turbulent with steamboats and fringed with cities. Yet here is a mountain in its centre but few feet have ever trod, or will tread for a century to come.

We designed to encamp as near the summit as we could, and obtain firewood, so that we might see the sun rise from the summit, but the heavens grew darker every moment, warning us to find shelter for the night. About 5 o'clock we left the top and went helter-skelter down the precipitous sides. After going at a break-neck pace for several miles over rocks, along ravines and through the bushes, S——th shouting at every leap "*go-in-down*," we at length stopped and began to peel bark to cover us for the night, for we were twelve miles from a clearing, and it was getting dark. Soon the axe resounded through the forest, and tree after tree came to the earth to furnish us fuel. "Every man must pick his own bed," cried our guide; for he had his hands full to erect a shanty. Our knapsacks were laid aside, and we scattered ourselves among the balsam trees with knife in hand to cut boughs to sleep on. The mossy ground was damp, and I picked me a thick couch and stretched myself upon it while supper was preparing. Our fire was made of logs more than twenty feet long, and as the flames arose and caught the spruce trees they shot up in pyramids of flames, crackling in the night air like so many fire-crackers. One dry tree took fire, and I asked if it might not burn in two during the night and fall on us. Cheney walked around it to ascertain the way it leaned, then quietly seating himself said, "yes, it will burn in two, but it will fall t'other way." I must confess, this cool reply was not wholly satisfactory, for burning trees sometimes take curious whims,—however, there was no help, and so I lay down to sleep. The storm which had been slowly gathering soon commenced, and all night long the rain fell, but the good fire kept crackling and blazing away, and I was so completely fagged out that I slept deliciously. I awoke but once, and then enjoyed such a long and hearty laugh, that I felt quite refreshed. The immense logs in front of us, became in time a mass of lurid coals sending forth a scorching heat. Hence, as we lay packed together like a row of pickled fish, those in the centre took the full force of the fire. First a sleeper would strike his hand upon his thigh and roll over—then give the other a slap, dreaming, doubtless, of being boiled like a turkey, till at length the heat waked him up, when he rose and shot like an arrow into the woods. The next went through the same operation—the third, and so on, till all but the two "outsiders," of which I was one, were in the woods cooling themselves off in the rain. Not a word was spoken for some time, for they were not fairly awake, but as one began to ask another, why he was out there in the dark, the answers were so honest and yet so droll, that I went into convulsions. If you had heard them comparing notes as I did, back of the shanty, your sides would have ached for a fortnight. And then the sheepish way they crawled back one after another, looking in stupid amazement at me rolling and screaming on the balsam boughs, would have quite finished a soberer man than you.

The tramp of twelve miles, next morning, was the hardest, for the distance, I ever took. Stiff and lame, with nothing to excite my imagination, I dragged myself sullenly along, and at noon reached the Iron Works.

> "Oh, but a weary wight was he,
> When he reached the foot of the dogwood tree."

VII.

SAGACITY OF THE HOUND—THE INDIAN PASS—PRECIPICE TWO THOUSAND FEET HIGH.

BACKWOODS, July 6.

DEAR H——:

THE famous Indian Pass is probably the most remarkable gorge in this country, if not in the world. On Monday morning, a council was called of our party, to determine whether we should visit it, for the effects of the severe tramp two days before, had not yet left us, and hardly one walked without limping—as for myself, I could not wear my boots and had borrowed a pair of large shoes. But the Indian Pass I was determined to see, even if I remained behind alone, and so we all together started off. It was six miles through the forest, and we were compelled to march in single file. At one moment skirting the margin of a beautiful lake, and then creeping through thickets, or stepping daintily across a springing morass, we picked our way until we at length struck a stream, the bed of which we followed into the bosom of the mountains. We crossed deer paths every few rods, and soon the two hounds Cheney had taken with him, parted from us, and their loud deep bay began to ring and echo through the gorge.

The instincts with which animals are endowed by their Creator, on purpose to make them successful in the chase, is one of the most curious things in nature. I watched for a long time the actions of one of these noble hounds. With his nose close to the leaves, he would double backwards and forwards on a track, to see whether it was fresh or not—then abandon it at once, when he found it too old. At length, striking a fresh one, he started off; but the next moment, finding he was going back instead of forwards on the track, he wheeled, and came dashing past on a furious run, his eyes glaring with excitement. Soon his voice made the forest ring; and I could imagine the quick start it gave to the deer, quietly grazing, it might have been, a mile away. Lifting his beautiful head a moment, to ascertain if that cry of death was on *his* track he bounded off in the long chase and

Ingham. Burt.

ADIRONDACK PASS.

bold swim for life. Well; let them pass: the cry grows fainter and fainter; and they—the pursued and the pursuer—are but an emblem of what is going on in the civilized world from which I am severed. Life may be divided into two parts—the hunters and the hunted. It is an endless chase, where the timid and the weak constantly fall by the way. The swift racers come and go like shadows on the vision; and the cries of fear and of victory swell on the ear and die away, only to give place to another and another. Thus musing, I pushed on;—at length, we left the bed of the stream, and began to climb amid broken rocks that were piled in huge chaos, up and up, as far as the eye could reach. My rifle became such a burden, that I was compelled to leave it against a tree, with a mark erected near by, to determine its locality. I had expected, from paintings I had seen of this Pass, that I was to walk almost on a level into a huge gap between two mountains, and look up on the precipices that toppled heaven high above me. But here was a world of rocks, overgrown with trees and moss—over and under and between which we were compelled to crawl and dive and work our way with so much exertion and care, that the strongest soon began to be exhausted. Caverns opened on every side; and a more hideous, toilsome, breakneck tramp I never took. Leaping a chasm at one time, we paused upon the brow of an overhanging cliff, while Cheney, pointing below, said, "There, I've scared panthers from those caverns many times; we may meet one yet: if so, I think he'll remember us as *long as he lives!*" I thought the probabilities were, that we should remember *him* much longer than he would us. At least I had no desire to task his memory, being perfectly willing to leave the matter undecided. There was a stream somewhere; but no foot could follow it, for it was a succession of cascades, with perpendicular walls each side hemming it in. It was more like climbing a broken and shattered mountain, than entering a gorge. At length, however, we came where the fallen rocks had made an open space around, and spread a fearful ruin in their place. On many of these, trees were growing fifty feet high, while a hundred men could find shelter in their sides. As the eye sweeps over these fragments of a former earthquake, the imagination is busy with the past—the period when an interlocking range of mountains was riven, and the encircling peaks bowing in terror, reeled like ships upon a tossing ocean, and the roar of a thousand storms rolled away from the yawning gulf, into which precipices and forests went down with the deafening crash of a falling world. A huge mass that then had been loosened from its high bed, and hurled below, making a cliff of itself, from which to fall would have been certain death, our guide called the "Church,"—and it did lift itself there like a huge altar, right in front of the main precipice that rose in a naked wall more than a thousand feet* perpendicular. It is two thousand feet from the summit to the base, but part of the chasm has been filled with its own ruins, so that the spot on which you stand is a thousand feet above the valley below, and nearly three thousand above tide water. Thus it stretches for three-quarters of a mile—in no place less than five hundred feet perpendicular. By dint of scrambling and pulling each other up, we at last succeeded in reaching the top of the church, while from our very feet rose this awful cliff that really oppressed me with its near and frightful presence. Majestic, solemn and silent, with the daylight from above pour-

* Some say a thousand, others twelve hundred.

ing all over its dread form, it stood the impersonation of strength and grandeur.

I never saw but one precipice that impressed me so, and that was in the Alps, in the Pass of the Grand Scheideck. I lay on my back filled with strange feelings of the power and grandeur of the God who had both framed and rent this mountain asunder. There it stood still and motionless in its majesty Far, far away heavenward rose its top, fringed with fir trees, that looked, at that immense height, like mere shrubs; and they, too, did not wave, but stood silent and moveless as the rock they crowned. ***Any*** motion or life would have been a relief—even the tramp of the storm; for there was something fearful in that mysterious, profound silence. How loudly God speaks to the heart, when it lies thus awe-struck and subdued in the presence of His works. In the shadow of such a grand and terrible form, man seems but the plaything of a moment, to be blown away with the first breath. Persons not accustomed to scenes of this kind, would not at first get an adequate impression of the magnitude of the precipice. Everything is on such a gigantic scale—all the proportions so vast, and the mountains so high about it, that the real individual greatness is lost sight of. But that wall of a thousand feet perpendicular, with its seams and rents and stooping cliffs, is one of the few things in the world the beholder can never forget. It frowns yet on my vision in my solitary hours; and with feelings half of sympathy, half of terror, I think of it rising there in its lonely greatness.

> "Has not the soul, the being of your life,
> Received a shock of awful consciousness,
> In some calm season, when these lofty rocks,
> At night's approach, bring down th' unclouded sky
> To rest upon the circumambient walls;
> A temple framing of dimensions vast.
> *   *   The whispering air
> Sends inspiration from the shadowy heights
> And blind recesses of the cavern'd rocks;
> The little rills and waters numberless,
> Insensible by daylight, blend their notes
> With the loud streams; and often, at the hour
> When issue forth the first pale stars, is heard
> Within the circuit of the fabric huge,
> One voice—one solitary raven, flying
> Athwart the concave of the dark blue dome,
> Unseen, perchance, above the power of sight—
> An iron knell! with echoes from afar,
> Faint and still fainter."

I will only add, that none of the drawings or paintings I have seen of this pass, give so correct an idea of it, as the one accompanying this description. We turned our steps homeward, and after having chased a deer into the lake in vain, reached the Adirondack Iron Works at noon. We had traveled twelve miles, a part of the way on our hands and knees.

I had received a fall in the pass which stunned me dreadfully, and made every step like driving a nail into my brain. Losing my footing, I had fallen backwards, and gone down head foremost among the rocks —a single foot either side, and I should have been precipitated into a gulf of broken rocks, from which nothing of myself but a mangled mass would ever have been taken. Stunned and helpless, I was borne by my friends to a rill, the cool water of which revived me

Yours, &c.,

VIII.

THE HUNTER CHENEY—ENCOUNTERS WITH A PANTHER—DEADLY STRUGGLE WITH A WOLF—A BEAR AND MOOSE FIGHT—SHOOTS HIMSELF.

BACKWOODS, July 12

DEAR H——:

You know one expects to hear of hunting achievements upon our western frontier, where the sounds of civilization have not yet frightened away the wild beasts that haunt the forest. But here in the heart of the Empire State is a man whose fame is known far and wide as the "mighty hunter," and if desperate adventures and hair-breadth escapes give one a claim to the sobriquet, it certainly belongs to him. Some ten or fifteen years ago, Cheney, then a young man, becoming enamored of forest life left Ticonderoga, and with his rifle on his shoulder, plunged into this then unknown, untrodden wilderness. Here he lived for years on what his gun brought him. Finding in his long stretches through the wood, where the timber is so thick you cannot see an animal more than fifteen rods, that a heavy rifle was a useless burden, he had a pistol made about eleven inches in length, stocked like a rifle, which, with his hunting knife and dog, became his only companions. I had him with me several days as a guide, for he knows better than any other man the mysteries of this wilderness, though there are vast tracts even he would not venture to traverse. Moose, deer, bears, panthers, wolves, and wild cats, have by turns, made his acquaintance, and some of his encounters would honor old Daniel Boone himself. Once he came suddenly upon a panther that lay crouched for a spring within a single bound of him. He had nothing but his gun and knife with him, while the glaring eyes and gathered form of the furious animal at his feet, told him that a moment's delay, a miss, or a false cap, would bring them locked in each other's embrace, and in a death-struggle. But without alarm or over-haste, he brought his rifle to bear upon the creature's head, and fired just as he was sallying back for the spring. The ball entered the brain, and with one wild bound his life departed, and he lay quivering on the leaves. Being a little curious to know whether he was not somewhat agitated in finding himself in such close proximity to a panther all ready for the fatal leap, I asked him how he felt when he saw the animal crouching so near. "I felt," said he coolly, "as if I should kill him." I need not tell you that *I* felt a little foolish at the answer, and concluded not to tell him that I expected he would say that his heart suddenly stopped beating, and the woods reeled around him; for the perfect simplicity of the reply took me all aback—yet it was rather an odd feeling to be uppermost in a man's mind just at that moment—it was, however, perfectly characteristic of Cheney.

His fight with a wolf was a still more serious affair. As he came upon the animal, ravenous with hunger, and floundering through the snow, he raised his rifle and fired; but the wolf, making a spring just as he pulled the trigger, the ball did not hit a vital part. This enraged her still more; and she made at him furiously. He had now nothing but an empty rifle with which to defend himself, and instantly clubbing it, he laid the stock over the wolf's head. So desperately did the creature fight, that he broke the stock into fragments without disabling her. He then seized the barrel, which, making a better bludgeon, told with more effect. The bleeding and enraged animal seized the hard iron with her teeth, and endeavored to wrench it from his grasp—but it was a matter of life and death with Cheney, and he fought savagely. But, in the meantime, the wolf, by stepping on his snow-shoes as she closed with him, threw him over. He then thought the game was up, unless he could make his dogs, which were scouring the forest around, hear him. He called loud and sharp after them, and soon one—a young hound—sprung into view: but no sooner did he see the condition of his master, than he turned in affright, and with his tail between his legs, fled into the woods. But, at this critical moment, the other hound burst with a shrill savage cry, and a wild bound, upon the struggling group. Sinking his teeth to the jaw bone in the wolf, he tore her fiercely from his master. Turning to grapple with this new foe, she gave Cheney opportunity to gather himself up, and fight to better advantage. At length, by a well-directed blow, he crushed in the skull, which finished the work. After this he got his pisto made.

You know that a bear always sleeps through the winter. Curled up in a cavern, or under a fallen tree, in some warm place, he composes himself to rest, and, Rip-Van-Winkle-like, snoozes away the season. True, he is somewhat thin when he thaws out in the spring, and looks voracious about the jaws, making it rather dangerous to come in contact with him. Cheney told me, that one day, while hunting on snow shoes, he suddenly broke through the crust, and came upon a bear taking his winter's nap. The spot this fellow had chosen, was the cavity made by the roots of an upturned tree. It was a warm, snug place; and the snow having fallen several feet deep over him, protected him from frosts and winds. The unceremonious thrust of Cheney's leg against his carcass, roused up Bruin, and with a growl that made the hunter withdraw his foot somewhat hastily, he leaped forth on the snow. Cheney had just given his knife to his companion, who had gone to the other side of the mountain to meet him farther on; and hence, had nothing but his pistol to defend himself with. He had barely time to get ready before the huge creature was close upon him. Unterrified, however, he took deliberate aim right between the fellow's eyes, and pulled the trigger; but the cap exploded without discharging the pistol. He had no time to put on another cap; so, seizing his pistol by the muzzle, he aimed a tremendous blow at the creature's head. But the bear caught it on his paw with a cuff that sent it ten yards from Cheney's hand, and the next moment was rolling over Cheney himself in the snow. His knife being gone, it became simply a contest of physical strength; and, in hugging and wrestling, the bear evidently had the advantage; and the hunter's life seemed not worth asking for. But, just then, his dog came up, and seizing the animal from behind, made him loosen his hold, and turn and defend himself. Cheney then sprang to his feet, and began to look around for his pistol. By good luck he saw the breech just peeping out of the snow. Drawing it forth, and hastily putting on a fresh cap, and refastening his snow-shoes, which had become loosened in the struggle, he made after the bear. When he and the dog closed, both fell, and began to roll, one over the other down the side-hill, locked in the embrace of death. The bear, however, was too much for the dog, and, at length, shook him off, leaving the latter dreadfully lacerated—"torn," as Cheney said, "all to pieces. But," he added, "I never saw such pluck in a dog before. As soon as he found I was ready for a fight he was furious, bleeding as he was, to be after the bear. I told him we would have the rascal, if we died for it; and away he jumped, leaving his blood on the snow as he went. 'Hold on,' said I, and he held on till I came up. I took aim at his head, meaning to put the ball in the centre of his brain; but it struck below, and only tore his jaw to pieces. I loaded up again, and fired, but did not kill him, though the ball went through his head. The third time I fetched him, and he was a bouncer, I tell you." "But the dog, Cheney," said I; "what became of the poor, noble dog?" "Oh, he was dreadfully mangled. I took him up, and carried him home, and nursed him. He got well, but was never good for much afterwards—that fight broke him down." I asked him if a moose would ever show fight. "Yes," he said, "a cow moose, with her calf; and so will any of them when wounded or hard pushed. I was once out hunting, when my dog started two. I heard a thrashing through the bushes, and in a minute more I saw both of them coming right towards me. As soon as they saw me they bent down their heads, and made at me at full speed The bushes and saplins snapped under them like pipe-stems. Just before they reached me, I stepped behind a tree, and fired as they jumped by The ball went clear through one, and lodged in the other."

Cheney kills about seventy deer per annum. He has none of the roughness of the hunter; but is one of the mildest, most unassuming, pleasant men you will meet with anywhere. Among other things, he told me of once following a bear all day, and treeing him at night when it was so dark he could not see to shoot; then sitting down at the root, to wait till morning that he might kill him. But, after awhile, all being still, he fell asleep, and did not wake till daylight. Opening his eyes in astonishment, he looked up for the bear, but the cunning rascal had gone. Taking advantage of his enemy's slumbers, he had crawled down and waddled off. Cheney said he never felt so flat in his life, to be outwitted thus, and by a bear.

With one anecdote illustrating his coolness, I will bid his hunting adventures adieu. He was once hunting alone by a little lake, when his dogs brought a noble buck into the water. Cocking his gun, and laying it in the bottom of the boat, he pulled after the deer, which was swimming boldly for his life. In the eagerness of pursuit, he hit his rifle either with his paddle or foot, when it went off, sending the ball directly through one of his ankles. He stopped, and looking at his benumbed limb, saw where the bullet had come out of his boot. The first thought was, to return to the shore; "the next was," said he, "I may *need that venison before I get out of these woods*;" so, without waiting to examine the wound, he pulled on after the deer. Coming up with him, he beat him to death with his paddles, and pulling him into the boat, rowed ashore. Cutting off his boot, he found his leg was badly mangled and useless. Bandaging it up, however, as well as he could, he cut a couple of crotched sticks for crutches, and with these walked *fourteen miles* to the nearest clearing. There he got help, and was carried slowly out of the woods. How a border-life sharpens a man's wits. Especially in an emergency does he show to what strict discipline he has subjected his mind. His resources are almost exhaustless, and his presence of mind equal to that of one who has been in a hundred battles. Wounded, perhaps mortally, it nevertheless flashed on this hunter's thoughts, that he might be so crippled that he could not stir for days and weeks, but starve to death there in the woods. "I may need that venison before I get out," said he; and so, with a mangled bleeding limb, he pursued and killed a deer, on which he might feed in the last extremity.

IX.

GAME—MOOSE—CRUSTING MOOSE—A CATAMOUNT—CHASE BETWEEN A DEER AND A PANTHER—A BEAR CAUGHT IN A TRAP.

BACKWOODS, July 14, 1846.

DEAR H——:

GAME of all kinds swarm the forest; bears, wolves, panthers, deer, and moose. I was not aware that so many moose were to be found here: yet I do not believe there is an animal of the African desert with which our people are not more familiar than with it. In *size*, at least, he is worthy of attention, being much taller than the ox. You will sometimes find an old bull moose *eight feet high*. The body is about the size of a cow, while the legs are long and slender, giving to the huge bulk the appearance of being mounted on stilts. The horns are broad, flat, and branching, shooting in a horizontal curve from the head. I saw one pair from a moose that a cousin of Cheney killed, that were nearly *four feet* across from tip to tip, and the horn itself fifteen inches broad. The speed of these animals through the thick forests, seems almost miraculous, when we consider their enormous bulk and branching horns. They seldom break into a gallop, but when roused by a dog, start off on a rapid pace, or half trot, with the nose erect and the head working sideways to let their horns pass through the branches. They are rarely, if ever, taken by dogs, as they run on the start twenty miles without stopping, over mountains, through swamps, and across lakes and rivers. They are mostly killed early in the spring—being then unable to travel the woods, as the snow is often four and five feet deep, and covered with a thick sharp crust. At these times, and indeed in the early part of winter, they seek out some lonely spot near a spring or water-course, and there "yard," as it is termed: i. e. they trample down the snow around them and browse, eating everything clean as far as they go. Sometimes you will find an old bull moose "yarding" alone, sometimes two or three together. When found in this state, they are easily killed, for they cannot run fast, as they sink nearly up to their backs in the snow at every jump.

Endowed, like most animals, with an instinct that approaches marvelously near to reason, they have another mode of "yarding," which furnishes greater security than the one just described. You know that mountain chains are ordinarily covered with heavy timber, while the hills and swelling knolls at their bases are crowned with a younger growth, furnishing buds and tender sprouts in abundance. If *you* don't, the *moose* do; and so, during a thaw in January or early spring, when the snow is from three to five feet deep, a big fellow will begin to travel over and around one of these hills. He knows that "after a thaw comes a freeze;" and hence, makes the best use of his time. He will not stop to eat, but keeps moving until the entire hill is *bi*-sected and *inter*-sected from crown to base with paths he himself has made. Therefore, when the weather changes, his field of operations is still left open. The crust freezes almost to the consistency of ice, and yet not sufficiently strong to bear his enormous bulk; little, however, does he care for that: the hill is at his disposal, and he quietly loiters along the paths he has made, "browsing" as he goes—expecting, most rationally, that before he has finished the hill, another thaw will come, when he will be able, without inconvenience, to change his location. Is not this adapting one's self to circumstances?

But it is no child's play to go after these fellows in midwinter; for the places they select are remote and lonely. It generally requires one to be absent days, and from the more open settlements, weeks, to take them. The hunters lash on their great snow-shoes, which, like an immense webbed foot, keep them on the surface; and taking a sled and blankets with them, start for some deep, dark, and secluded spot which these animals are known to haunt. By night they sleep on the snow, wrapped in their blankets; and when they draw near the place where they expect to find a "yard," the utmost circumspection is used, and every advance made with the stealthiness of an Indian. Sometimes a moose will wind his enemies, and then he is all agitation and excitement; but the fatal bullet ends at once his troubles and fears, and his huge carcass is cut up, and the choicest parts carried home on the sled or sleds. Many a crimson spot is thus left on the snow in this wilderness, around which at night the wolves and panthers gather, filling the solitude with their cries.

Two Indians killed eighteen in this region last spring, and one hunter told me that he had shot three in a single day in the early part of March. These enormous wild cattle are of a black color, and when closely pressed, will fight desperately. Wolves have fine picking in deep snow, especially when there is a stiff crust on the surface. The slender hoof of the deer, which yard like the moose, cuts through at every leap, letting them up to the belly without giving firm ground to spring from, even then; while the broad-spreading paw of the wolf supports him and he skims along the surface. In this unequal chase, he soon overtakes his victim, and devours him. "But the wildest chase I ever saw," remarked a hunter to me once, with whom I was in the forest several days, "was between a panther and a deer, in the open woods." They were not fifteen feet apart, he said, when they passed him, and such lightning speed he never before witnessed. Though he had his rifle in his hand, and they were but a few rods distant when he saw them, he never thought of firing.

They came and went more like shadows than living

things. The mouths of both were wide open, and the tongue of the deer hanging out from fatigue, while their eyes seemed starting from their sockets—one from fear, the other from rage. Swift as the arrow in its flight, and as noiseless, save the strokes of their rapid bounds on the leaves—they fled away, and the forest closed over them. Over rocks, and logs, and streams, that slender and delicate form went flying on, winged with terror, while, so near that he almost felt his hot breath on his sides, he heard his foe pant after him. Ah, hunger will outlive fear, and before many miles were sped over, that harmless thing lay gasping in death, and its entrails were torn out ere the heart had ceased to beat.

And thus, methought, it happens everywhere in God's universe. Innocence is safe nowhere :—even in the solitude of the forest—in nature's sacred temple—it falls before the power of cruel passion. The hunters and the hunted come and go like shadows, and the appealing accents of fear, and the fierce cry of pursuit or vengeance, ring a moment on the ear, and then are lost in a solitude deeper than that of the wilderness.

The panther like the lion depends more upon his first spring than any after effort. Lying close to a limb, he watches the approach of his victim; then with a single bound lights upon its back, planting his claws deep in the quivering flesh. It requires a strong effort then to shake him off, or loosen his hold.

His cry of hunger is very much like that of a child in distress, and is indescribably fearful when heard at night in the forest. It is seldom, however, that a traveler sees any of these animals of prey. They are more afraid of him, than he of them; and winding him at a long distance, flee to their hiding places. It is only in winter that they are dangerous. I have often, however, roused them up by my approach. I once heard a catamount scream in a thick clump of bushes not a hundred yards from me—it was just at twilight, and made me bound to my feet as if struck by a sudden blow, and sent the blood tingling to the ends of my toes and fingers. You have heard of electrical shocks, galvanic batteries, etc.—well, their effects are mere slight nervous stimulants compared to the wild, unearthly screech of a catamount at night in the woods. This fellow was not satisfied with one yell, but moving a little way off, coolly squatted down and gave another and another, as if enraged at our proximity, yet afraid to confront us. They will smell a human form an inconceivable distance.

On another occasion, if I had had a dog with me, I should have brought you home a bear skin as a trophy. I was passing through a heavy windfall, where berry bushes, &c., had grown up over the fallen timber, when I suddenly heard a hoarse "humph, humph," and then a crashing through the bushes. I had come upon a huge bear which was quietly picking berries. The fellow put off at a tremendous rate, and I after him. I should judge he was about three hundred yards distant at the outset, which he soon increased to four hundred. He made for a swamp which he probably crossed, and climbed up the steep mountain on the farther side to his den.

When he went down the bank to the swamp, he showed the size of his track, and he must have been a rouser. With a dog I should have "treed" him, and then he could have been easily shot. The hunter with me caught one a short time before, in a trap, on this same mountain. Where two large trees had fallen across each other so as to make an acute angle, he placed a piece of meat, and a strong spiked steel trap directly in front of it, covered over with leaves

The bear of course could not get at the meat without first stepping over the trap, and as bad luck would have it, he stepped *in*. The trap was not fastened in its place, but attached by a chain to a long stick —the old fellow therefore traveled off till the clog caught against a tree. I would not have supposed it possible that a bear could make such rending work with his teeth as he did. For six feet upward from the root, the tree against which he was caught, was not only peeled of its bark, but the hard fibres were torn away in large splinters, while the clog itself was all chewed up, and the ground around furrowed, in his struggles and rage.

Beavers were once found in abundance here, and Cheney says he knows where there is a colony of them now. Otter and sable are now and then taken, but trappers are fast exterminating the fur tribe. Yet for game and fish there is no region like it on the continent.

Yours truly,

X.

LAKE HENDERSON—A JULY DAY—A SUNSET, AND EVENING REVERIE.

My Dear H——:

I am just recovering from the exhaustion of the last few days' tramping, and, quiet and renovated, enjoy everything around me. On the banks of Lake Henderson—a charming sheet of water—I have been reclining for hours, drinking in the fresh breeze at every inspiration. It is a summer afternoon, and I know by the atmosphere that veils these mountain tops, and the force of the sun when I step out of the shade, that it is a hot July day. At this very moment, while I am stretched at my ease, watching the still lake, and those two deer that for the last hour have

Gignoux. Burt.

been wading along the farther shore, drinking the cool water, and nibbling the long grass that skirts the bank, and lazily beating off the flies, you are sauntering up Broadway, or, perhaps, have just returned from a stroll in Union Park, and are wooing the sea breeze, that, entering the city at the Battery, is gently diffusing itself through every street and alley. Ah, that sea breeze is the only salvation of New York. After a hot, panting day, when the fiery pavements and red brick walls have concentrated and redoubled the heat, how refreshingly, and like a good angel, comes that, at first slight, but gradually increasing sea-wind, to the fevered system. Moist from its long dalliance with the salt waves, its kiss is soft and welcome as that of a —— I beg your pardon, I meant to say, as a doctor once remarked to me, "it is a very pleasant stimulant." Yet I know Broadway is looking like a furnace just cooled off; and with all your windows and doors thrown open, you are still languid, while a sultry and oppressive night awaits you. I pity you from my heart; you have been in Wall street the whole of this scorching day, and have not drawn a breath below your throat, for the air you live on was never made for the lungs.

You are pale and exhausted, while now and then comes over you, a sweet vision of rushing streams and waving tree tops, and cool floods of air. I see you in imagination, flung at full length upon the sofa, and hear that expression of impatience which escapes your lips. But here it is delicious—my lungs heave freely and strongly, and every moment refreshes instead of enervates me. Before me spreads away this beautiful lake, shaped like a tea leaf, while all along the green shores and up the greener mountain side, there is a barely perceptible motion among the leaves, as if they were so many living things stirring about upon a carpet of velvet. Farther on, the Adirondack Pass lifts its startling cliff into the air, and farther still the solemn mountains stand bathed in the splendor of the departing sun. The placid surface before me is now and then broken by the leap of a trout as some poor fly ventures too near where he swims—but all else is still and calm. Oh, that I could catch the shadows of thoughts and feelings that flit over me. There is an atmosphere of beauty around my spirit, that fills me with a thousand sweet but vague visions.

There is something I would grasp and retain, but cannot—would speak, but have not the power to utter it. The soul is powerless to act and,

> "Dizzy and drunk with beauty, reels
> In its fullness."

Just look at the glorious orb of day as it rolls down that distant mountain slope, into the gorge which seems made on purpose to receive it. Lower and and lower sinks the fiery circle, till at last it disappears, leaving an ocean of flame where it stood, while dark shadows begin to creep over the lake and shores. On the mountains, there is a bright line of light which slowly ascends as if striving to linger around the loveliness below. Inch by inch it creeps upward, growing brighter as it rises, till at length the highest summit is reached—irradiated and forsaken. Its last baptism was on that bald peak which blazed up a moment like an altar-fire to God, then sunk in darkness—and now the pall of night is slowly drawn over all.

Thus, my friend, did this July evening pass with me, and with a sigh over the gorgeous dream that had vanished, I turned away. Though the night was

5

lovely with its stars and sky, which seemed doubly brilliant in contrast with the black mountain masses that shut out half the heavens; yet the dash of a stream over its broken channel, and the hoot of the distant owl conspired to give a loneliness to the scene the former could not enliven. I thought of home, and those I loved—of life and its lights and shadows—of death and its deeper mysteries—of the far world beyond the stars, and that "palace" to which "even the bright sun itself is but a porch lamp."

But these reveries will not fit me for to-morrow's toil, and so good-night to you.

Yours truly.

XI.

TAHAWUS WITH THE CLOUDS BELOW IT—A HARD TRAMP—A PLANK BED ON THE BOREAS RIVER—A SORRY COMPANY TRAVELING AFTER A BREAKFAST.

BACKWOODS, July.

DEAR H——:

THERE is a path across the mountains to the road that leads into the centre of this vast plateau, and to the lake region. But I am going out to a settlement before I start for that still more untrodden field, filled with scenes far more beautiful. This is the last morning I shall, probably, ever look on the summit of Tahawus. You cannot conceive what an affection one has for a majestic old mountain few have ever ascended, and on whose top he himself has stood. For six years not a foot has profaned this almost inaccessible peak, and I feel as if I had paid a visit to a hermit and left him in his solitude, thinking over the interview which had broken up the monotony of his existence.

Clouds are rolling around him to-day, and I think of what Prof. Benedict, of Burlington, told me. He ascended it once for scientific purposes, and made experiments on the top which have been of great service to the State. He said that the spectacle from it one morning in a northeast storm, was sublime beyond description. *He* was in the clear sunlight, while an ocean of clouds rolled on below him in vast white undulations, blotting out the whole creation from his view. At length, under the influence of the sun, this limitless deep slowly rent asunder, and the black top of a mountain emerged like an island from the mighty mass, and then another and another, till away, for more than three hundred miles in circumference, these black conical islands were sprinkled over the white bosom of the vapory sea. The lower portions of the mountains then appeared, while the mist collected in the deep gulfs, and lay like a vast serpent over the bed of a river, that wound through the forest below, or shot up into fantastic shapes, resembling towers and domes, and cliffs, and clouds, forming, and shifting, and changing in bewildering confusion. It is impossible to conceive anything half so strange and wild.

It seemed as if

> "A single step had freed one from the skirts
> Of the blind vapor—opened to the view
> Glory beyond all glory ever seen
> By waking sense, or by the dreaming soul.
> *   *   *   *   *   *
> Oh, 'twas an unimaginable sight;
> Clouds, mists, streams, waters, rocks, and emerald turf;
> Clouds of all tincture, rocks, and sapphire sky,
> Confused, commingled, mutually inflamed,
> Molten together, and composing thus,
> Each lost in each, a marvellous array
> Of temple, palace, citadel, and huge
> Fantastic pomp of structure without name,
> In fleecy folds voluminous enwrapped.
> Such by the Hebrew prophets were beheld
> In vision—forms uncouth of mightiest power,
> For admiration and mysterious awe."

We had engaged a teamster to come on a certain day and take us out to the settlements. He, however, did not make his appearance; and so, after a fatiguing tramp of twelve miles in the morning, we concluded to set out on foot, hoping to meet him somewhere in the woods. But in this we were disappointed, and therefore traveled on until the shades of evening began to gather over the forest, admonishing us to seek a place of rest for the night. We had now gone sixteen miles from Adirondack, which, added to the twelve miles in the morning, made nearly thirty miles —a severe day's work. Twilight brought us to the Boreas River, and here we found a log shanty, which some timber cutters had put up the winter before, and deserted in the spring. It was a lonely looking thing, dilapidated and ruinous, with some straw below, and a few loose boards laid across the logs above by way of a chamber. I expected to have had some trout for supper, for a young clergyman who had joined us a day or two before, said that on his way up he took sixteen out of one pool as fast as he could cast his line. But it was nearly dark when we reached the river, and so, kindling a blazing fire outside, we dined on our last provisions, and turned in. As I said, only a few boards were laid across the logs above, leaving the rest of the loft perfectly open. By getting on a sort of scaffolding, and reaching the timbers overhead, we were able to swing ourselves up on the scanty platform. After I succeeded in gaining this perch, I helped the others up; but the clergyman was rather too heavy, and just as he had fairly landed on the boards, one gave way, and down he went. I seized him by the collar, while he, with one hand fastened to my leg, and with the other grasped a timber, and thus succeeded in arresting his fall, and probably saved himself a broken limb.

We lay in a row on our backs along this frail scaffolding, filling it up from end to end, so that, if the outside ones should roll a half a yard in their sleep, they would be precipitated below. A more uncomfortable night I never passed; and after a short and troubled sleep, I lay and watched the chinks in the roof, for daylight to appear, till it seemed that morning would never come. I resolved never again to abandon my couch of leaves for boards, and a ruined hut through which vermin swarmed in such freedom, that I dreamed I had turned into a spider, and speculated a long time on my unusual quantity of legs, endeavoring in vain to ascertain their respective uses.

At length the welcome light broke slowly over the still forest, and I turned out. Huge stones and billets of wood hurled on the roof soon brought forth the rest of our companions, and we started off. We had nothing to eat, and seven weary miles were to be measured before we could reach the nearest clearing. What with the night I had passed, and that seven miles' tramp on an empty stomach, I was completely knocked up. The clear morning air could not revive me—my rifle seemed to weigh fifty pounds—my legs a hundred and fifty, and I pushed on, more dead than alive. At length we emerged into a clearing, and there, in a log hut, sat our teamster, quietly eating his breakfast. The day before, he had started through the forest; but becoming frightened at the wildness and desolation that increased at every step, had turned back—choosing to leave us to our fate rather than run the risk of making a meal for wolves and bears. I could have seen him flogged with a good will, I was so indignant. Hungry, cross, and weary, we sat down to breakfast, and then stowed ourselves away into a lumber wagon, and rode thirty miles to our respective stopping-places. The little settlement seemed like a large village to me, and the inhabitants the most refined I had ever met.

Several days' rest here has restored me, and I begin to feel my system rally, and am conscious of strength and vitality to which I have been a stranger for six months.

I shall remain here a few days, and then start for the lake region—the only land route to which is a rude road ending at Long Lake. The Adirondack chain subsides away there into more regular ridges—it is, however, wilder than the region I have left, and we shall have to rely for food on what we ourselves can catch and kill.

Yours truly,

XII.

A THUNDER STORM—A SOLUTION OF LIFE.

BACKWOODS, July 12.

DEAR E——:

THUNDER storms are not particularly pleasant things in the woods, but you are now and then compelled to take them. I have just passed through one, and, like all grand exhibitions of nature, they awaken pleasure in the midst of discomfort. I have never witnessed anything sublime, even though dangerous, that did not possess attractions, except standing on the deck of a ship in the midst of a storm, and looking off on the ocean. The wild and guideless waves running half-mast high, shaking their torn plumes as they come—the turbulent and involved clouds—the shrieks of the blast amid the cordage, and groans of the ship, combine to make one of the most awful scenes in nature. Yet I loathe it and loathe myself as I stand or *try* to stand, reeling to and fro, holding on to a belaying pin or rope, for support. But give me firm footing, and I love the sea. I don't believe Byron ever thought of writing about it till he got on shore. The idea of a man thinking, much less making poetry while he is staggering like a drunken man, is preposterous.

But I like to have forgot myself—I was reclining on the slope of a hill the other day, near a lake, from which I had a glorious view of the broken chain of the Adirondack. From the ravishing beauty of the scene, my mind, as it is wont, fell to musing over this mysterious life of ours—on its strange contrasts and stranger destinies, and I wondered how its selfishness and sorrow, blindness and madness, pains and death, could add to the glory of God; or how angels could look on this world without turning away, half in sorrow and half in anger, at such a blemished universe, when suddenly, over the green summit of the far mountain, a huge thunder-head pushed itself into view. As the mighty black mass that followed slowly after, forced its way into the heavens, darkness began to creep over the earth. The song of birds was hushed—the passing breeze paused a moment, and then swept by in a sudden gust, which whirled the leaves and withered branches in wild confusion through the air. An ominous hush succeeded, while the low growl of the distant thunder seemed forced from the deepest caverns of the mountain.

I lay and watched the gathering elements of strength and fury, as the trumpet of the storm summoned them to battle, till at length the lightning began to leap in angry flashes to the earth from the dark womb of the cloud, followed by those awful and rapid reports that seemed to shake the very walls of the sky. The pine trees rocked and roared above me —for wrath and rage had taken the place of beauty and placidity—and then the rain came in headlong masses to the earth. Keeping under my shelter of bark, I listened to the uproar without, as I had often done under an Alpine cliff in the Oberland, waiting for the passage of the storm. In a short time its fury was spent, and I could hear its retiring roar in the distant gorges. The trees stopped knocking their green crowns together, and stood again in fraternal embrace, while the rapid dripping of the heavy rain drops from the leaves, alone told of the deluge that had swept overhead. I stole forth again, and but for this ceaseless drip, and the freshened look of everything about me in the clearer atmosphere, I should hardly have known there had been a change.

Scarce a half hour had elapsed—yet there the blue sky showed itself again over the mountain where the dark cloud had been—the sun came forth in redoubled splendor, and the tumult was over. Now and then a disappointed peal was heard slowly traveling over the sky, as if conscious it came too late to share the conflict; but all else was calm, and tranquil, and beautiful, as nature ever is after a thunder-storm. But while I lay watching that blue arch, against which the tall mountain, now greener than ever, seemed to lean; suddenly a single circular white cloud appeared over the top, and slowly rolled into view, and floated along the radiant west. Bathed in the rich sunset—glittering like a white robe—how beautiful! how resplendent! A moving glory, it looked as if some angel-hand had just rolled it away from the golden gate of heaven. I watched it till my spirit longed to fly away and sink in its bright foldings. And then I thought were I in the midst of it, it would be found a heavy bank of fog—damp and chill like the morning mist, which obscures the vision and ruffles the spirit, till it prays for one straggling sunbeam to disperse the gloom. But seen at that distance—shone upon by that setting sun—how glorious! And here, methought, I had a solution of my mystery of life. With its agitations and changes—its blasphemies and songs—its revelries and violence—its light and darkness—its ecstasies and agonies—its life and death—so strangely blent—it is *a mist, a gloomy fog*, that chills and wearies us as we walk in its midst. Dimming our prospect, it shuts out the spiritual world beyond us, till we weep and pray for the rays of heaven to disperse the gloom. But seen by angels and spiritual beings from afar—*shone upon by God's perfect government and grand designs of love*—it may, and doubtless does, appear as glorious as that evening cloud to me. The brightness of the throne is cast over us, and its glory changes this turbulent scene into a harmonious part of his vast whole. "God's ways are not as our ways, neither are his thoughts as our thoughts." After it has all passed, and the sun of futurity breaks on the scene, light and gladness will bathe it in undying splendor.

I turned away with that summer cloud fastened in my memory forever, and thankful for the thunder-storm that had taught my heart so sweet a lesson.

Yours truly,

——.

XIII.

A RIDE THROUGH THE FOREST—A LEAN DINNER—CHENEY'S COUSIN—SWIMMING A LAKE WITH HORSES.

BACKWOODS, August.

DEAR H——:

I AM off again for the woods—resolved to penetrate to the heart of this wild country, whose scenery cannot be matched this side of the Alps. For fifty miles, we can with care go on horseback, and then we must be our own beasts of burden.

Our company consists of five—a young clergyman, whom I persuaded to try bivouacking in the forest, instead of lounging at Saratoga Springs for his health, R—ffe, formerly a merchant in Maiden Lane, but now a thorough backwoodsman, cutting down forests and putting up mills, &c., and Doctor T—ll, and young P——

It was a bright morning, as, mounted on fresh

horses, with our rifles on our shoulders, we passed from the more open settlements, which gradually grew thinner and wilder, and entered the unbroken forest. In the trouble we were at to obtain an extra horse, and afterwards a saddle, we forgot to take provisions for the way; so, after traveling for nearly thirty miles, we found ourselves on the banks of the Boreas River, (our old friend, with whom we encamped a week or two since, some thirty miles to the north-east,) weary and hungry, and twelve miles of forest to the nearest clearing. It was now one o'clock, and we had been in the saddle since early in the morning. Our horses needed food and rest, so did we; but the former was easier obtained for our beasts than for us. Taking off their saddles and tying them head and foot to prevent them from straying away, we turned them loose, to browse in the forest. W—d hunted around for berries to allay his hunger, while the doctor smoked his pipe and chewed spruce gum which he peeled from the trees, by way of stomach-stayers. R—ffe and myself thought of trying the trout; but the heavily timbered and tangled banks forbade all access to the stream except by plunging in. Hungrier than I ever remember to have been before, I floundered through the woods down the stream, seeking in vain for an opening; until, driven to desperation, I jumped in. But fly fishing with a crooked and green stick is rather unsatisfactory business, and though raising some twenty, I succeeded in taking only one, and he of small dimensions. Just as I had got him nicely stowed away in my pocket, a rifle shot—the signal to return—called me back. When I reached our resting place, I found my companions all in the saddle and ready for departure. "What!" said I, "are you going?" "Yes, let us hurry on!" "Not I," I replied, "till I devour this trout, for between my long ride and fast, and the effort to catch him, I am on the extreme limit of starvation. Come, doctor, strike me a fire while I dress him." So the doctor kindled a blaze, while I cut off the trout's head on a stone, and spitted him on a stick, ready for roasting. A few minutes in the blaze rendered him fit for my not over-nice palate, and I chewed him with a vigor I had never before exhibited, and when his tail finally disappeared, I heaved a sigh like one whose days of happiness are over. I looked around in despair, for there was nothing else eatable to be seen; so mounting my steed, I pushed on after the rest of the company.

Straggling on in Indian file, we went in a sort of hurry scurry through the woods, saying nothing, but each one evidently aware that he could not get to a supper too soon. Over mountains and across swamps, through a break in the Adirondack chain, which we here again struck; we urged on our jaded animals, with naught but the rush of the wild bird's wing, and the scared look of the pheasant or the deer, as he hurried from our path, to break the monotony of the ride. Yet this traveling along a narrow path in the forest is a right kingly march. Only think of riding all day through a magnificent colonnade, the columns lifting a hundred feet above your head, and crowned with Corinthian capitals, made after a richer model than the acanthus leaf. How the soul awakes in this new existence, and casting off the fetters that has bound it, rejoices in broader liberty, and leaps with a new, exultant feeling. The green, moving arch over your head does not confine you as it sheds down its freshness and fragrance on the path, for it reveals between its glorious fret-work of leaves and twigs a limitless dome beyond, that carries away the soul to farther, freer, brighter regions. Oh! how I love the glorious woods, and the sense of freedom they bring. How can one stay where he is cheated, exasperated, slandered, and mortified, when he has the broad forest to rejoice in, and such companions only as his own choice may select?

Towards night, we came to a clearing, the five families of which composed the entire town. Just before sunset, our host, a cousin of Cheney, and myself, went to a lake close by, on the opposite shore of which two deer were quietly grazing. Stepping into a boat, we endeavored to get within shot, but a loon a little way off, kept up such a loud and continual scream, that they were more than usually cautious, and soon moved away. Cheney had a huge black dog with which I became on the most intimate terms, much to the surprise of his master who declared he had never before seen him so playful with a stranger. I told him I did not doubt it, for hunters had often made the same remark to me, but that I prided myself on only one quality—the power to win the love of children and dogs. He said he was an excellent dog for bears, and only a few months before attacked one on the side-hill opposite the house, and kept him at bay all day. Soon as Bruin attempted to run he would fasten on his haunches, thus compelling him to turn and fight. Cheney was away at the time—but on returning at evening, he heard his dog barking furiously in the woods, and taking down his rifle, went to him, and shot the bear.

Next morning we plunged again into the forest, and as we rode along, I noticed trees at certain intervals, marked "H," which, after vainly attempting to account for, I finally enquired the reason of. "Oh, it means *highway*," was the reply. This was a rather comical mode of telling one he was on the highway, still I was thankful for the information. In another place we came upon fires built over a huge rock in the middle of the track, compelling us to take a semicircle in the woods. On inquiring the cause of this, to me, singular procedure, I was told that settlers, hired by the State, were working on the road, and in the absence of drills, took this method of breaking the rocks to pieces. Being sand-stone, the fire slowly crumbled them apart, so that the crowbar or lever could remove them. I thought of Hannibal, and his fire and vinegar on the rocks of the San Bernard; and men seemed going back to their primitive state. Instead of cutting down the trees that stood in the way, they hewed off the roots, and then hitching a rope to the tops, pulled them over with oxen. And thus they work and toil away here in the woods—yet not wholly heedless of the great world without. How strange it seems to behold men thus occupied—living contentedly fifty miles from a post office or village—and hear their inquiries about the war with Mexico, asking of events that have been forgotten months ago in New York!

The path grew rapidly worse as we proceeded—in some places endangering the limbs of our animals, and indeed our own necks. Sometimes we were up to the girths in a morass, and again leaping a huge tree—but at last we arrived at Long Lake, and it was *literally reaching* the *end* of the journey. The path as we approached the shore, had dwindled to a mere Indian-trail, and there entirely disappeared. With no road around, and no sign of life in sight, save a solitary log hut on the farther side of the lake, we waded up and down the shore till stopped by the rocks—looking in vain for some way of escape. Just then a flock of wild ducks shot out of a small bay at our feet, when crack! crack! went our rifles. The next moment a boat put off from the opposite shore, rowed by a boy. "Where is the path," was our inquiry as he approached, "that leads along the lake to some clearing?" "You can't go," was the reply, "there hain't none." "But what shall we do with our horses?" "I don't know."—After planning awhile, we concluded to fasten them in the woods, and bring over grass in the boat. So, tying them to the trees, and hanging our saddles on the branches, we crossed over. With all Hamilton County for a stable, our jaded animals passed the first night.

But carrying provender across the lake took up too much time, and therefore the next morning we concluded, after a long consultation, to swim them over. W——d first rode his powerful black horse, which the day before, by his amazing strength, had saved him from a broken neck or limb, into the lake. The noble animal was accustomed to the swamps and the forest, but not to deep water, and he sunk almost to his ears. W——d, somewhat frightened, as he found himself submerged to the armpits, began to pull sharply on the rein, which brought the horse nearly perpendicular in the water, with his fore feet pawing the air. The more erect the poor animal stood, the harder he was forced to pull the rein to keep from sliding off. Looking up, I saw his danger—for, thrown backward so by the bit, the struggling animal would, in a minute more, have fallen over upon him. I shouted out, " Let go the rein instantly, and grasp the mane!" He did so, and the horse relieved from the strain on his head, righted himself and brought his rider safely to the shore. In swimming the lake, however, he sunk to his ears, and groaned and grunted with every stroke. Another would not swim at all; but the moment he got beyond his depth, flung himself upon his side compelling us to hold his head on the stern of the boat and tow him across. The rest took to their work more kindly, especially a sorrel mare, which swam without an effort—the ridge of her back just skimming the surface, and her motion easy and steady as that of a swing.

We were right glad to reach the opposite forest;—and dragging our dripping beasts up the rocky bank, threaded our way to the only hut we had seen since morning

Yours, &c.

XIV.

CAMPING GROUND—MITCHEL THE INDIAN GUIDE—TROUT FISHING ON A LARGE SCALE—NIGHT.

LONG LAKE, Aug. 10.

DEAR H——:

LET me introduce you to our camp. It is a little after noon, and a most lovely day, and there, at the foot of the lake, back a few rods, in the forest, is burning a camp-fire. On a stick that is thrust into the ground and leans over a log, hangs a small kettle of potatoes—a little one side is suspended to a tree a noble buck just dressed, some of the nicest bits of which are already roasting in a pan over the fire. In a low shantee, made of hemlock bark, entirely open in front, lazily recline the young clergyman and the doctor, watching with most satisfied looks the cooking of the savory venison. On the other side are stretched the weary hounds in profound slumber. An old hunter is watching, with knife in hand, the progress of a johnny-cake he is baking in the ashes, giving every now and then a most comical hitch to his waistbands while, as if to keep up the balance, one whole side of his face twitches at the same time. Close by him is my Indian guide whom I obtained yesterday, coldly scrutinizing my new modeled rifle. Taciturn and emotionless as his race always are, he neither smiles nor speaks.

Knowing that his curiosity was excited, I remarked, "Mitchell, I wish you would try my rifle, for I have some doubts whether it is perfectly correct." Without saying a word, he took up an axe, and going to a distant tree struck out a chip, leaving a white spot. Returning as silent as he went, he raised my gun to his face, where it rested for a moment immovable as stone, then spoke sharp and quick through the forest. The bullet struck the white spot in the centre. He handed back the rifle without uttering a word—that shot was a better comment on its correctness than anything he could say.

Our venison and johnny-cake and potatoes were at length done ; and each of us peeling off a bit of clean hemlock bark for a plate, we sat down on the leaves, and placing our bark dishes across our legs, with a sharp stick in one hand for a fork, and our pocket knives in the other, commenced our repast. I have dined in palaces, hotels, and amid ancient ruins, but never so right royally before. We were kings here, with our rifles by our side, and no one to dispute our sway; and then such a palace of countless columns encompassing us, while the gentle murmur of the tiny wave as it laid its cheek on the smooth pebbles below, made harmony with the refreshing breeze that rustled in the tree tops and lifted the ashes of our already smouldering camp fire. I thought last winter, at the Carlton House, that the venison made a dish that might please a *gourmet*, but it was tasteless, savorless, compared to *this* venison, cut off from the freshly killed carcass, and roasted in the open forest. A clear stream near by furnished us with a richer beverage than wine; while the fresh air, and gleaming lake, and sweet islands sleeping on its bosom, gave to the spirits a healthier excitement than society.

After the repast was finished, we stretched ourselves along the ground and smoked our cigars, and talked awhile of trout and deer and bears and wolves and moose. At length the Indian arose and made preparations for departure. Taking our rifles and fishing tackle, we pushed our boats into the lake, and made for Raquette River, the outlet of the lake, and thence into Cold River.

I wish I could give you some conception of this stream. At this season of the year it is almost as moveless as a pond, while its waters are clear as fluid crystal, revealing a smooth and pebbly bottom. The shores of both the rivers are all trodden over with moose and deer and bear tracks. During the afternoon we had endeavored to take some trout, of which Mitchell told me the river was full. But the unruffled surface of the stream, combined with its pellucid waters, and an unclouded sun, made every fish fly to his lurking place long before we got sight of him. Under the deep shadow of an overhanging and wooded bank, Mitchell at length took one, while I had the pleasure of seeing a two pounder rise to my fly with open mouth and dilated eyes; but just as he was going to snap it, he caught a glimpse of us, and darted like a flash of lightning to the bottom, from whence no after-coaxing could lure him. But as the sun went down I had better success. Being the only one who used a fly, I took all the trout. They were, however, of a small size and difficult to hook, for I had nothing but a common pole cut from the forest, on which to rig my line. I had left my light and delicate rod in the settlements, as I should advise every one to do, who endeavors to penetrate this pathless region. When one is compelled to carry his own rifle, overcoat, and underclothing, and sometimes his cooking utensils, and that, too, with a walk of twenty miles on a stretch before him, he would do well not to lumber himself up with fishing rods.

But when the sun at length totally disappeared behind the mountains, and the surface of Cold River, overshadowed by an impenetrable forest, became black as ink, the trout left their retreats; and in a short time the water was in a foam with their constant leaping. Where but a short time before we had passed, looking down through the clear depths without seeing a single finny rover, now there seemed an innumerable multitude. Here a sudden bold bound—there a long shoot as a fierce fellow swept along after a large fly, kept the bosom of the stream in a bubble. The Indian and my companions had stiff poles, cord lines, and large hooks, with a piece of raw venison for bait. This they would "*skitter*" along the surface, and the moment it caught the eye of a trout, away he would rush with a leap and plunge after it. I found that my light tackle was entirely out of place in this new mode of fishing, for while I was drowning one big fellow, those in the boat with me would take half a dozen. Besides the time for fishing was short, for twilight had already settled on the forest—and so, after in my hurry breaking two or three snells, I, too, rigged on a cord line, big hook, and piece of venison. I never saw anything like it in my life—it was a constant leap, roll, and plunge there around our lines—and some of them such immense fellows for brook trout. In a half an hour we took at least a half a bushel, many of them weighing three pounds, and few less than a pound.

At length, however, it became too dark to fish, and a single rifle shot of the Indian recalling our scattered boats, we started for the camp.

Turning the head of our boat, we drifted down to Raquette River, and then pulled for the lake. This was a mile of hard rowing, and it was late before we reached the outlet. One skiff having started sooner than we, was already at the camp—the cheerful fire of which burst on us through the trees as we rounded a point of the outlet, and shot upon the bosom of the quiet lake. "Look, R—ffe," I exclaimed, "yonder is the camp fire, and now another light moves down to the beach, where they are dressing the trout for supper." He sprang to the oars, and the light boat fled like a wild deer toward that cheerful flame. Islands and rocks flew by, and under a cloudless sky, and myriads of bright and glorious stars, we sped gaily on, till, at length, the boat grated on the pebbly beach, and a joyous shout that made the solemn old forest ring, went up from the camp and shore. In a moment all was bustle and preparation for supper, and the noblest dish of trout I ever ate I took there by fire light in the woods. My appetite, it is true, was sharp, and we made a sad inroad into our pile of fish.

After supper we lay around in every variety of attitude upon the dry earth, lazily snuffing up the fragrance of the woods, and looking off on the still surface of the lake in whose clear depths the stars of heaven stood trembling, and listening to wild hunting stories, interspersed now and then with flashes of broad humor, till at length the deep breathing of the

Indian admonished us that we, too, needed repose to prepare us for the toils of the next day. We did not retire to our rooms and blow out the lights, but spreading a blanket on the earth and leaves, stretched ourselves upon it in a row, and with our feet to the blazing fire, composed ourselves to rest—that is, all the party but myself. I sat up for some time by the crackling fire, and watched the others as they dropped one after another to sleep, until exhausted and weary, I also stretched myself beside the Indian with a log for my pillow, between two knots of which I placed my head to keep it from rolling.

A little after midnight I awoke—the wind had shifted to the east, and was blowing strong and chill, sending a rapid swell on the beach, and a loud murmur though the cedar tops overhead. The fire had died away, except a few smouldering brands, while the bright stars, those ceaseless watchers, looked kindly down from their high sentinel posts in heaven. The wild and lonely scream of the northern diver, came at intervals through the darkness, as he floated far away on the water; and night, solemn night, with the great forest, was around me. I strolled down to the lake shore, and let the breeze fall on my fevered head, while the glimmer of the dying embers of our camp-fire through the trees rendered the scene doubly lonely. I returned, and seizing the axe, soon had a bright and crackling fire sending its light over the sleepers. The sparks, borne higher and higher by the wind, danced about in the forest, and shed a clear light on a noble white hound that lay sleeping in careless ease at the foot of a tree. Tall trunks stood column-like and still, on every side—gradually growing dimmer and dimmer, till lost in a mass of blackness, and contrasting strangely with the motion and roar of the tops, through which the wind swept in fitful gusts. Again I stretched myself on the ground, and woke no more till light was dawning in the east, and then with a shudder and start as though a tomahawk were gleaming over my head. The Indian's dog had crawled upon me, and lay heavily along my body, his head resting on my bosom, his mouth to my mouth, while a low growl which issued from his chest, startled the Indian by my side. I never was so struck with the alertness of an Indian. I am not slow to wake myself, especially in a case like this; but before I opened my eyes, Mitchell was on his feet; and as I looked up, I saw him standing over me with his piercing black eye fixed on the dog. "Be still!" he exclaimed, and then, as if talking to himself, added, "it is strange, but he is watching you, he smelt danger." His keen nose probably winded some wild animal prowling about our camp—attracted hither by the savory smell of venison. I gently caressed the noble fellow, and rose from my hard couch. The whole group were standing listlessly around the fire, yawning and stretching, while the few jokes that were cracked created only a mockery of laughter.

Yours truly.

XV.

A CAMP SCENE IN THE MORNING—A SHOT AT AN EAGLE —A DEER CHASE.

LONG LAKE, August 1.

DEAR H——:

MY last left us yawning and stretching around our camp fire a little after daylight in the morning, looking and feeling stupid and heavy—but a fresh wash in a mountain rill near by restored us to life, while the answers to the inquiries how each other had slept, brought back the merriment that seldom flags in the woods. "Well, R—ffe, how did *you* sleep?" "Pretty well, only H— kept punching me to keep me off from him." "And how did you sleep, H—?" "As I'll never sleep again. I was on the lower hill-side, and served as a block to the whole of you. You rolled down against me and wedged me in so tight that I couldn't, with my utmost effort, turn over, to save my life." "Mr. W—d, was you broke of your rest?" "No: I slept pretty well, considering the circumstances." Turning to Mr. P—, I remarked, "Well, Mr. P—, I saw you get up once when I rose to put some wood upon the fire. You lay rolled up in your blanket like a mummy, while the sparks from the fire fell in a shower upon you. I thought you would find it rather too hot before morning." "I don't remember getting up at all," he replied; "probably the roaring fire you made *did* cause the smoke to choke me. I never waked but once, and then I was startled by the sound of an axe; I opened my eyes, and saw you splitting down the stump—the root of which I had made my pillow—directly over my head." This, of course, I stoutly denied, amidst the uproarious laugh of the company. I then remembered the frightened look he gave me, as I was cutting into a stump near by him, and in the next moment roll rapidly in his blanket down the hill. The suddenness and oddity of the movement surprised me at the time, but now it was all explained. In his half-wakened state, he saw the bit of my axe gleaming in the fire light, and thought it was descending directly on his skull. No wonder he performed those sudden evolutions!

At length Mitchell having finished his pipe, called to the hounds, "Come, Rover, come Maj," and with shouldered rifle moved down to the shore. The night before, as we sat around the camp fire, we bid for the first fire at the deer we should start in the morning. I outbid the rest, when Mitchell dryly remarked, "I'll take you in *my* boat." He had not forgotten his promise, or rather the reward, and so beckoning to me, we started off. After rowing a mile or two, we landed the old hunter and the dogs, who soon disappeared in the forest. Just then, Mitchell pointed to a lofty pine tree, towering above the surrounding forest, on an upper limb of which sat a grey eagle in her nest. "I believe I'll try to get a shot at her," said he, and started off. With the stealthiness of his race, he crept and dodged through the woods till I thought he never *would* shoot. I watched the noble bird through my glass, and could see her head ever and anon turn quickly as she heard the snapping of a stick, or rustling of a leaf, which Mitchell with all his care could not prevent, till, at length, rising on her nest, she cast her piercing eye on every side, and then detecting the danger, gathered her strong pinions and soared away. Wheeling round and round the place of her young, she finally stooped on the top of an immense pine tree. Again and again she rose and circled away, and then alighted where she could overlook her offspring. She had discovered the Indian, but the love of her young was stronger than her fear, and she would not leave them. At length the sharp crack of a rifle rang though the woods, and the noble bird, unscathed, rose and sailed over where I stood. I lifted my rifle and again let it fall, saying to myself, "This time, at least, you shall not fall a victim to parental love." Mitchell soon joined me, and I remarked, "Well, you missed her." "Yes, it wants close squinting to pick one off from the top of such a pine as that."

Pushing off, we rowed over to an island where we could have a fair view of the lake on every side, and awaited the deer; and here I felt some of the miseries of a hunter's life. A cold east wind swept the bosom of the lake, and I sat and shivered, thinking there would be vastly more poetry in staying by the camp-fire, and eating venison already killed, than waiting for that which was yet running on the mountain. Mitchell climbed a cedar and stood looking over the broken top to catch the first cry of the hounds as they opened on the track, while I sat with my back against a hemlock, my rifle across my lap, and my coat collar turned up over my ears, wishing it was over with, and thinking the while of breakfast, as my eye turned ever and anon, most wistfully down the lake, where R——ffe was rowing backwards and forwards from the camp to a rock in the water, on which we had spread our venison, killed the day before. The dry east wind proved too strong—the dogs could not follow the scent, and soon appeared again, trotting along the shore with the hunter.

It was not long after this, before I was discussing a noble trout, that lay, fresh from the pan, along my bark plate.

After breakfast, our little fleet of three skiffs, was launched, and we paddled slowly up the lake. In the mean time, the east wind, which always poisons me, died away, and this beautiful sheet of water lay like a mirror in which the blue heavens were quietly gazing on their own beauty. After rowing two or three miles, Mitchell remarked it was a good time to start a deer. I hailed the boats, and in a few minutes we were in close consultation as to the best mountain on which to put out the dogs. "Anywhere," said P——, "will fetch one; but that mountain (pointing to the left,) is the best, for the echo of the cry of the hounds comes down from it in grand style. I want H—— to hear the echo of the chase along its sides once,—it is more blood-stirring than the sound of a trumpet." Sending one boat on a mile and a half a head, and one back, Mitchell and myself landed the hunter and dogs and took a middle station. They had scarcely reached the shore, before the dogs opened. Pushing back into the lake, I saw the white hound appear on the beach at a little distance, shoot backward and forward a few moments with his nose to the ground, then utter a loud deep cry. "Ah," said I to myself, "that has started at least *one* 'noble stag,' from his couch of leaves, and he stands this moment with dilated nostril and extended neck, while a pang of terror, shoots through his wild heart as the yell again ringing through the forest, tells him that the voice is on his track."

The west wind had now risen, and we sat and rocked on the waves, listening to the furious outcry that the mountain sent down to the water. The green forest shut in both hounds and deer, but you could follow the chase by the rapidly flying sound along the steep acclivities. How earnest and eager is the bay of a blood-hound on a fresh track—ah, it was exciting, cruel as it may seem to some. Suddenly the boat, a mile and a half above us, shot out like an arrow, from behind a rock, and flew over the water. The quick eye of the Indian caught it, and exclaiming "the deer has took to the water there," sprang to his oars. "It is not possible," I replied; "it is scarcely half an hour since the dogs started." He stopped, rose to his full length in the boat—stood for a moment like a statue, then dropping on his seat, he exclaimed, "it is," and seized the oars. I did not deem it possible he could discover it that distance with his naked eye, but he had been trained from infancy in the forest. In that short time such a change had passed over the man, that I scarcely knew him. Taciturn, slow and indolent in his movements, I had not thought him capable of sudden excitement. But now the energy and fire of ten men seemed concentrated in him. His strokes fell with a rapidity and power I had never before witnessed. I have seen men row for wagers and for dear life; but never saw blows tell on a boat as did those of his.

It is true the skiff was light, for it was made to be carried on one man's shoulders across the country from lake to lake—it is true also, that I threw myself on the paddle with which I steered, with all the strength I was master of; but the strokes of Mitchell seemed each time to lift the cockle-shell from the lake. As he fell back on the oars, so rapid was the passage of the boat, that the water, as it parted before it, rose up on each side as high as his shoulders, and foamed like a torrent past me. On, on we sped like a winged creature, when a rifle shot rang dull and heavy in the distance, and the wind lifting the smoke bore it down towards us. "Did he hit him?" exclaimed Mitchell. I dropped my paddle and lifting my glass to my eye, replied, "No, and it is a buck. I see his antlers, and he is bearing right down on us. Pull, pull away my brave fellow." He *did* pull, and so did I, and we flew over the surface. The other boat had been compelled to lay-to a moment to mend an oar, which had given us the advantage, but it was now again sent with no stinted strokes down the lake. At length I could see the head and antlers of the noble buck, as with dilated nostrils and terror-stricken glance, he swam and doubled on his pursuers. "Hold," I exclaimed, as he glanced away towards the shore. The boat fell into the trough of the waves just as I raised my rifle to my shoulder, and the little cockle-shell rocked so like mad on the water, and my frame was quivering so with the exhausting effort of the last few minutes, that the muzzle of my piece described all sorts of mathematical diagrams around the head of the deer, as I endeavored to make it bear for a single second upon it. I could not shoot—but "fire! fire!" shouted Mitchell, and "fire" it was. The bullet struck just under his throat, throwing the water over his head, while he made a desperate spring and pulled for the shore. Shame on me, but I might as well have shot on horseback under a full gallop.

At that moment the other boat flew like a spirit

past, and crack went the rifle of W—d. He missed, and again our skiff was rapidly dividing the waves before her, while in scarcely more time than I have been relating it, another ball was in my gun, and I exclaimed, "Now, Mitchell, as we approach him, throw the head of the boat on the waves so the motion shall be steady, and if I miss him I will fling my rifle into the lake." As we came up, a single stroke of the oar sent her round, and as she rose and fell on the short sea, I "watched my time" and pulled. A desperate plunge and a bloody streak upon the water, told that the bullet had found the life-blood. Struggle on, bold fellow, but your life is reached, and never again shall your foot press the mountain-side! Just then another shot struck the water close by our boat, glanced, and also entered the deer. He bowed his antlered head in the waves, and turned over on his side, while the short, convulsive efforts told of his death agony. A few strokes of the oar, and our boat lay alongside—the knife of the Indian entered his throat, and the deed was done. I raised him by the horns, and towed him slowly along toward the shore. The excitement of the chase was over, and as I gazed on the wild, yet mild and gentle eye of the noble creature, now glazing in death, a feeling of remorse arose in my heart. I could have moralized an hour over the beautiful form as it floated on the water. The velvet antlers (they are now in their velvet) gave a more harmless aspect to the head than the stubborn horn, and I almost wished to recall him to life. It seemed impossible that, a few minutes before, that delicate limbed creature was treading in all the joy of freedom his forest home. How wild had been his terror, as the fierce cry of the hound first opened on his track! —how swift the race down the mountain side, and how free and daring his plunge from the rock into the wave! How noble his struggles for life. But the bold swimmer had been environed by foes too strong for him, and he fell at last, where he could not even turn at bay. The delicate nostril was relaxed in death, and the slender limbs stiff and cold.

I was awakened from my moralizing by Mitchell, who that moment ceased rowing and gave a call. The gallant white hound had followed the track of the deer to the water, where he stood perplexed and anxious till the first rifle shot fell over the lake. He then plunged in, and had ever since been swimming after us in the chase. We lay-to, and took the noble fellow in and then pulled for shore

XVI.

A MAGNIFICENT PROSPECT—FOURTEEN HOURS WITHOUT FOOD.

OWL'S HEAD, August 5

DEAR H——:

HAVE you ever been on the summit of the Righi, in Switzerland? It is said to command the finest view in that land of magnificent prospects. I once stood on its top, and saw the sun come up in his glory, till forests, lakes, rivers, and villages sprang into life and beauty, and the whole range of the Bernese Alps, from Sentis to the Jungfrau, glittered in red and gold, while the vast snow fields slept in deep shadow between.

My eye never opened on a more glorious panorama, and I stood amid its surpassing beauties in silent amazement. The view, it is said, embraces a tract of country three hundred miles in circumference, with eleven lakes in sight from the summit, though I never could make out more than half that number. The Righi has become almost a classic name, while the "Owl's Head," from which I date my letter, has never yet dared to show its face in civilized life. Indeed, the cognomen has been given by a man wandering by, from its shape, and it waits a new christening. A forester here has requested me to give it a name, promising it shall keep it. If you will send me one, I will see to the baptism, and you shall have the honor of naming a mountain; which is far more imposing than giving a name to a baby. It deserves a good one, for insignificant as it may seem, to plant your feet on an "owl's head," it looks off on a prospect that would make your heart stand still in your bosom. Look away toward that distant horizon! In its broad sweep round the heavens, it takes in nearly four hundred miles, while between slumbers an ocean —but it is an ocean of tree tops. Conceive, if you can, this vast expanse stretching on and spreading away, till the bright green becomes shaded into a deep black, with not a sound to break the solitude, and not a hand's breadth of land in view throughout the whole. It is a vast forest-ocean, with mountain-ridges for billows, rolling smoothly and gently on like the subsiding swell of a storm. I stand on the edge of a precipice which throws its naked wall far down to the tops of the fir trees below, and look off on this surpassingly wild and strange spectacle. The life that villages, and towns, and cultivated fields give to a landscape is not here, neither is there the barrenness and savageness of the view from Tahawus. It is all vegetation—luxuriant, gigantic vegetation; but man has had no hand in it. It stands as the Almighty made it, majestic and silent, save when the wind or the storm breathes on it, waking up its myriad low-toned voices, which sing

> "The wild profound eternal bass
> In nature's anthem."

Oh, how still and solemn it slumbers below me; while far away yonder, to the left, shoot up into the heavens the massive peaks of the Adirondack chain, mellowed here, by the distance, into beauty. Yet there is one relief to this vast forest solitude—like gems sleeping in a moss bed, lakes are everywhere glittering in the bright sunshine. How calm and trustingly they repose on the bosom of the wilderness! Thirty-six, a hunter tells me, can be counted from this summit, though I do not see over twenty.

There, like a snake crawling out from the mountain gorge, comes Long Lake, with its glittering head—and yonder is Forked Lake, and farther on Raquette Lake—and farther still, Great and Little Tuppers Lake, and away, a mere luminous point—but I will cut short the list, for, indeed, many have no names. Some of these are from four to six miles in width, and yet they look like mere pools at this distance, and in the midst of such a mass of green.

I have gazed on many mountain prospects in this and the old world, but this and the view from Tahawus have awakened an entirely new class of emotions. They are American scenes, constituting one of the distinctive features of our country, where nature seems to have formed everything on such a large model, merely because she had so much room to work in. I wanted to set fire to the trees on the summit of the mountain, so as to present an unobstructed view, but the foliage was too green to burn. A deep moss bed covered the whole top, on which we reclined as on the softest couch. You will get some conception of the wildness of the country, when I tell you that it took us nearly five hours to *find* this mountain after we *first came in sight of it,* though at the time not more than two miles distant, in a straight line, from its base. We rowed six miles and landed with its blue top in clear view—then took the direction with our pocket compasses, and started off. One who had been to the summit before acted as guide, but after circling round one or two swamps, and falling unconsciously out of our way, by following ridges that *seemed* to go in the direction we wished, we found ourselves wholly at loss. Hills and swamps, and a dense forest on every side, completely obstructed our view, and we stumbled on hour after hour, and ascended two mountains, before we could finally get another glimpse of the one we were after. We breakfasted about six in the morning, and had left our fishing-tackle on the shore, where we expected to be again by noon, and take some trout for dinner—but it was half-past three when we reached the top of this mountain, making nine hours of the most desperate toil; with nothing to eat, and, what was worse, with no prospect of getting anything till we should again reach our boats. The doctor was in perfect despair, and declared he could not return without food. As a last resort, he took from his pocket a piece of venison he had brought along for trout bait, (a Frenchman could not have wished it *older*,) and devoured it. I begged the half of a cigar of one of the company, (I offered him five dollars for the whole of it,) to stimulate my exhausted system, and we began our descent. We again lost our course and wandered about till, wearied out, and hungry, we sat down in a bed of wild "sheep sorrel," and plucked the green leaves and ate them. An owl fluttered on a branch over head, and I drew up my rifle and fired, but missed him. I verily believe, if I had killed him I should have eaten him on the spot. The doctor declared he would not stir—he would rather die than go any further. We cheered him up with the remembrance of his *venison*, at which he made sundry wry faces, not to be mistaken, and which drew peals of laughter from us, weary and faint as we were. The doctor would then stagger on, but it was really pitiful to look back and see him stop, put his shoulder to a tree, and sink his head against the trunk, then slide down in utter exhaustion, on the green moss at the root.

At length the rifle shot of the clergyman, who had gone on while we tarried for the doctor, announced that he had at last found the lake. This gave new life to our spirits, and we scrambled joyously forward. Those slender boats never looked so beautiful to me before, as they then did, resting quietly on the beach.

It was now nearly dark, and the nearest hut was four miles off. Three of us sat down in one boat and looked despairingly on each other, as much as to say, "Who *can* row these four miles?" Invalid as I was, I seemed to have the most strength left, and so took the oars and rowed two miles and a half, though every stroke seemed to tear out my very stomach—ribs and all. We at length moored our skiff at the base of a hill, and began the ascent to a clearing. With both hands on the muzzle of my rifle, which I used as a pole to push myself along with, I dragged one foot after another, till I at length stopped, and bowing my head on my gun, declared I was fairly done up, and could go no farther. Just then there came a flash of lightning that set the dark forest in a blaze, followed by a peal of thunder that made the shores and mountains tremble, as it rolled like the report of a hundred cannon down the lake. I instinctively straightened up, as the thought flashed over me, what sort of a mathematical line the bullet of my rifle would just then have made through my brain, had the powder but ignited. I immediately stepped forward with considerable alertness, though not without reflecting on the wonderful power electricity and magnetism exerted over the human system, especially under such circumstances.

I at length reached the hut, with a head bursting with pain; and, throwing myself on the floor, begged most piteously for a morsel of bread. I had been *fourteen* hours without food, and most of the time undergoing the severest toil. That night was one of pain to me, and as I turned on my rude bed, I felt that for once I had "paid too dear for the whistle."

Yours truly.

XVII.

LONG LAKE—A FEARFUL NIGHT—A GALE IN THE WOODS—MAN BITTEN BY A RABBIT.

LONG LAKE, August.

MY DEAR H——:

You must expect now and then a hiatus in my journal, for hours of idleness are indulged in here as well as in civilized life. To-day, wearied with yesterday's tramp, we may be loitering around the camp, cleaning our rifles, and recruiting ourselves for a long to-morrow. Sometimes we idle away the entire morning, and spend the afternoon in fishing—again take a deer in the morning, and after dinner dress him, then perhaps, practice rifle-shooting towards evening. At another time a rain-storm sets in, which lasts two or three days, compelling us to keep close and do nothing. As these are all rather monotonous to me, the relation would be so to you—beside, one trout fishing and one deer hunt is very much like another; and though the excitement is ever new to him who is engaged in them, they have no freshness in the description.

Long Lake is one of the most beautiful sheets of water I ever floated over, and its frame-work of mountains becomes the glorious picture. No artist has ever yet visited it; and alas, as I have no skill with the pencil, its beauties, like the "rose in the wilderness," must, for a while, blush unseen. I never saw a more beautiful island than "Round Island," as it is called, situated midway of the lake. As you look at it from above or below, it appears to stand between two promontories, whose green and rounded points are striving to reach it as they push boldly out into the water; while, with its abrupt, high banks, from which go up the lofty pine trees, it looks like a huge green cylinder, sunk there endwise, in the waves. I wished I owned that island—it would be pleasant to be possessor of so much beauty.

Mitchell went yesterday to the foot of this lake to meet his father and sister, who were on the way to visit him. They had started some time before, a hundred and fifty miles distant, in a bark canoe, and he calculated that, that day or the next, they would be at the outlet. He not having returned, I thought in the afternoon I would row down and find him. I had some thirteen miles to go, and unfortunately, neither of the two young men with me could handle the oars or steer, so I stripped to the task. Luckily, however, there was a strong gale blowing down the lake, and I landed on an island and cut a bush, which I hung over with pocket handerchiefs to make it hold the wind, and then set it upright in the centre of the boat as a mainsail. The breeze was strong and steady, and worked admirably. Far away to the south-west, the golden sky shone in brilliant colors, and over its illuminated depths the fragmentary clouds went trooping as if joyous with life, while to the northwest, towards which our frail craft was driving, the heavens were black as midnight, and the retiring storm-cloud looked dark and fierce—retreating, though still unconquered. The sun was hastening to the ridge of the sky-seeking mountains, and his departing beams threw in still deeper contrast the black masses that curtained in the eastern heavens. But still the waves kept dancing in the light, as if determined not to be frowned out of their frolic, and it was with no little pleasure I saw that threatening cloud yield to the balmy and swift careering breeze that swept the bosom of the lake.

At length, just as we were glancing away from the head of a beautiful island, I saw a boat coming towards us, impelled against the wind by the steady strokes of a powerful rower. As it shot near, I beheld the swarthy and benevolent face of Mitchell. He lay on his oars a minute to hear my salutation and my proposition, then pointed to a deep bay a mile distant, around which stretched a white line of sand; and again bent to his oars. I followed after, for I knew there was his camp; and soon after our boats grated on the smooth beach, and we were sitting beside a bark shanty, and discussing our future plans. But those few barks, piled against some poles, were not enough to cover us, and soon every one was at work, peeling spruce trees, or picking hemlock boughs. The cloudless sun went proudly, nay, to me, triumphantly to his royal couch amid the mountain summits —and as twilight deepened over the wild landscape, our camp fire shot its cheerful flame heavenward, and we lay scattered around amid the trees in delightful indolence. Mitchell had caught some trout, and these, with the contents of our knapsacks, furnished us a noble supper. With my back against a stump, I held a splendid trout in one hand, while my hunting-knife in the other, peeled off his salmon-colored sides in most tempting, delicious morsels.

After supper I asked Mitchell if we could not get a deer before going to bed. He said yes, if the wind went down so that we could float them. This floating deer I will describe in another place, for there was no stirring out that night. The wrathful little swells came rushing furiously against the unoffending beach, the tall tree-tops swayed to and fro, and sighed in the blast—our roughly-fanned fire threw its sparks in swift eddies heavenward, and all betokened a wild and fearful night. "No boat must leave the beach," and so carefully loading our rifles and setting them up against the trees, we began to prepare for our night's repose. Some with their heads under the bark shanty, and their feet to the fire—others in the open forest, with their heads across a stick of wood—lay stretched their full length upon the earth. I lay down for a while, but the wind, which had increased at sunset, now blew furiously, filling the forest with such an uproar that it was with difficulty I could shake off the delusion that I was in the midst of t' ocean. I could not sleep, so rising from my couch of boughs, I went out and sat down on the ground, and looked and listened. The steady roar of the waves on the beach below mingled in with the rush of the blast above, the tall trees rocked and swung on every side, and flung out their long arms into the night —their leafy tresses streaming before them—and groaned on their ancient foundations with a deep and steady sound—till my heart was filled with emotions at once solemn and fearful. To add to the sublimity and terror of the scene, ever and anon came a dull and heavy shock, like the report of distant cannon. It was made by a tree falling all alone there, in the depths of the forest. Oh, what strange emotions those muffled echoes awoke within me. Sometimes I thought one of these gigantic forms near me, must also fall in the struggle, and crush some of our company into the earth; and then again forgetting the danger, my soul would bow to the lordly music, till that great primeval forest seemed one vast harp—its trunks and branches the mighty wires, and the strong blast the fierce and fearless hand that swept them. Now faint and far in the distance I could catch the coming anthem till, swelling fuller and clearer on my excited ear, it at length went over me with a sea-like roar, then died away in the far solitude. God seemed near me, there, in the fearful night, and His voice was speaking to me. How calm the sleepers around me lay in the firelight, reposing as quietly in the wild uproar, as if naught but the dews of heaven were gently distilling, and yet how helpless they appeared in their slumbers! God alone was their keeper, and I never felt more deeply the protection of that parental hand, than there at midnight.

The moon at length arose on the darkness, and the wind gradually lulled to a gentler motion. I threw myself on the ground, and watched the bright orb as it slowly mounted the heavens, with feelings I will not attempt to describe.

It was now about one o'clock, and I was endeavoring to compose myself to slumber, when there occurred one of those ludicrous incidents that makes one's romance vanish like mist, and yet derives half of its comicality from the time and circumstances in which it occurs. As my eyes were resting on the fine proportions of a young, athletic backwoodsman, who was lying near the smouldering brands on the open earth, his head resting across a stick of wood for a pillow, and his heavy breathing telling of the profoundest slumber, I saw a rabbit steal from the bushes and cautiously approach him. With his nose close to the ground, he smelt around until he came to the sleeper's brawny hand outstretched upon the leaves. Some fragments of the johnny-cake still clinging to his thumb, deceived the rabbit into the belief that the whole digit was edible, and he put his teeth into it. This wakened the backwoodsman, who, rising to a sitting posture, looked wildly around him and then examined his thumb. All was quiet there; and imagining he had, in his dreams, thrashed his hand about and struck a splinter, he fell back, and was soon fast asleep. After waiting a proper time, the rabbit stole forth again, and creeping cautiously up to the large greasy hand, made his teeth meet through it. This roused the poor fellow with a start, and he caught a glimpse of his assailant as, with his long ears laid flat on his back, he scampered into the bushes. K——g looked a moment at the place where he had disappeared, and then at his bleeding thumb, muttering in the mean while, "There, I've ketched you at it —now—you had better be off." The serious tone in which this was said, finished me, and I went into convulsions of laughter. The look of innocent wonder—the dreadful imprecation, and the surprise and terror of the poor rabbit, crouching far away in the bushes, combined so much of the "serio-comico," that I laughed till I awoke the entire camp, who inquired what was the matter. A loud shout followed the explanation, which gradually died away into silence, as one after another dropped to sleep again. I, too, at length sunk in slumber, and was just in the midst of a sweet dream, when "crack" went a rifle, not ten yards from me, sending me to my feet with a start. The poor rabbit, however, was the only sufferer B——n, after I had thus unceremoniously roused the camp, lit his pipe, and sitting down behind a stump, watched for the rabbit. Seeing him steal cautiously forth, he had put a bullet through him, and thus ended the innocent creature's existence.

At length the welcome morning appeared, and launching our boats, we started for Cold River to take some trout.

Yours truly.

XVIII.

TROUTING—A DUCK PROTECTING HER YOUNG BY STRATAGEM—SABBATH IN THE FOREST.

LONG LAKE, Aug

DEAR H——:

I BELIEVE I broke off my last letter to go a-fishing—well the Indian and myself went ahead, hoping to surprise some deer feeding in the marshes, but were disappointed. Reaching the foot of the lake, we shot noiselessly down the Raquette River, till we came to a huge rock that rose out of the bed of the stream, when we turned off and began to ascend Cold River. When we reached it, the surface was covered with foam bubbles, made by the constant springing of the trout after flies. They had absolutely churned it up, and for awhile our hooks brought them to the surface fast—but we were too late—the sun soon rising over the forest, shed such a flood of light on the water, and indeed *through* it, to the very bottom, that scarcely a fish could be coaxed from his hiding-place. Our boats and ourselves also threw strong shadows, sufficient to frighten less wary fish than trout. We however took enough for breakfast, and started for home. By the way, is it not a little singular that fish should eat their own flesh; the *first one we caught served as bait for the others.*

As we were returning, Mitchell left the main stream and entered a narrow and shallow channel, that by making a circuitous route, reached the lake close beside the outlet. Passing silently along, we roused up a brood of ducks among the reeds. The mother first took the alarm, and seeing at a glance that she could not escape with her young, left them and fluttered out, directly ahead of our boat. She then began to make a terrible ado, striking her wings on the water, and screaming, and darting backwards and forwards, as if dreadfully wounded and could be easily picked up. I instinctively raised my rifle to my shoulder: then thinking the shot might frighten the deer we were after, I turned to Mitchell and inquired if I should fire. "I guess I wouldn't," he replied; "she has young ones." My gun dropped in a moment. I stood rebuked, not only by my own feelings, but by the Indian with me. I was shocked that this hunter who had lived so many years on the spoils of the forest, should teach me tenderness of feeling. That mother's voice found an echo in his heart, and he would not harm one feather of her plumage; nor could the bribe be named that would then have induced me to strike the anxious affectionate creature. As I saw her thus sacrificing herself to save her young, provoking the death-shot in order to draw attention from them, I wondered how I could for a single moment have wished to destroy her. I leaned over the boat and watched her movements for nearly half a mile. She would keep just ahead of us, sailing backwards and forwards, now striking her wings on the water, as if struggling with all her strength to fly, yet unable to rise; and now screaming out as if distressed to death at her perilous position; yet cunningly moving off in the meantime, so as to allure us after, in order to increase the distance between us and her offspring. While we were near the nest, she swam almost under our bow; but as we continued to advance she grew more timorous, as if beginning to think a little more of herself. I could not blame her for this, for she had hitherto kept within reach of certain death if I had chosen to fire. But it was curious to observe in what exact proportion her care for herself increased as the danger to her offspring lessened. She would rise and fly some distance, then alight in the water, and await our approach. If she sailed out of sight a moment, she would wheel and look back, and even *swim* back, till she saw us following after, when she would move off again. The foolish thing really believed she was outwitting us, and, I have no doubt, had many self-complacent reflections on the ease with which ducks could humbug human beings. After we had proceeded in this way about half a mile, she rose into the air, and striking the Raquette River, sped back by a circular sweep to her young. As her form disappeared round a bend of the stream, I could not help murmuring, "Heaven speed thee, anxious mother." Ah, what a chattering there was amid the reeds when her shadow darkened over the hiding-place, and she folded her wings amid her offspring, and listened with matronly dignity to the story each one had to tell?

All this, however, was speedily forgotten as we emerged on the lake, whose bosom was swept by a strong wind, against which we were compelled to force our tiny skiffs as we pulled for the camp. It was now nine o'clock, and I never waited with so much impatience for a meal as I did for the johnny-cake that was slowly roasting amid the ashes. We had but one pan, and until the cake was done we could not cook our trout—and so stretched under the shadow of a huge stump, with my chip-plate in my hand, I lay and watched the crackling flames with all the philosophy I could muster.

Mitchell, however, acted on philosophy of another description, and while we were waiting for the pan, dressed a pound trout, and cutting a long limber stick, thrust one end of it through the fish lengthwise, and sticking the other end in the ground, placed it at a proper distance and angle over the fire. He then lay down near it to superintend the cooking, which after sundry changes and turns was completed. This I had seen him do before, but now came the perfection of laziness. Sitting up, he swung the stick around towards him, so that as he fell back on his elbow, the trout hung suspended over his head; and thus while it bobbed up and down, he quietly peeled off the delicious morsels and ate them. That grave, swarthy Indian stretched on the leaves, with the trout nodding above him, as he slowly stripped away the flesh, furnished a picture I should like to have taken.

After breakfast we had no dishes or forks to clean, but throwing them both away, wiped our knives on a chip, and in a moment were ready for a start. It was Saturday, and the heavens which had been so clear the night before, now began to gather blackness—the burdened wind moaned through the forest, or went sobbing over the lake that was every moment fretting itself into greater excitement, and everything betokened a gloomy and tempestuous day. We were fourteen miles from a human habitation; and though I expected that day to have gone thirty miles farther into the forest and spent the Sabbath, the storm that was approaching made the shelter of a log cabin seem too inviting, and I changed my mind. But to row fourteen miles against a head wind and sea was no child's play, and for one I resolved not to do it. So, making a bargain with Mitchell, the Indian, I wrapped my oil-skin cape about me, and laying my rifle across my lap, ensconced myself in the stern of the boat, and made up my mind to a drencher. The black clouds came rushing over the huge mountains, and the rain soon began to fall in torrents. Now hugging the shore to escape the blast, and now sailing under the lee of an island—once compelled to land till the hurricane had passed—we crawled along until at length, late in the afternoon, we found ourselves comfortably housed.

The log hut of Mitchell, in which I spent the Sabbath, was in the centre of two or three acres of cleared land ; all the rest was forest. During the day, I was struck with the sense of propriety, and delicacy of feeling shown by him. Sunday must have been a weary day to him, yet he engaged in no sports, performed no work, that I saw, inappropriate to it. In the afternoon, however, he took down his violin, and I expected such music as would distress one to hear on the Sabbath. But he refrained from all those tunes I knew he preferred, and played only sacred hymns, most of them Methodist ones. I could not imagine where he had learned them ; but this silent respect for my feelings made me love him at once, and I conceived a respect for him I shall never lose.

The day went out in storms, and as I lay down that night on my rough couch, I could hardly believe I was in the same State of which New York was the emporium, whose myriad spires pierced the heavens.

I have been thus particular, because in no other way can you get a correct idea of the *daily* life one is compelled to lead who would penetrate these wilds. It is nonsense to talk of dignity, and the impropriety of a man's carrying a rifle and fishing-tackle, and spending his time in shooting deer and catching trout. Such folly is becoming to him only, who sits on the piazza of a hotel at Saratoga Springs, at the expense of twelve dollars a week for his health. I love nature and all things as God has made them. I love the freedom of the wilderness and the absence of conventional forms there. I love the long stretch through the forest on foot, and the thrilling, glorious prospect from some hoary mountain top. I love it, and I know it is better for me than the thronged city, aye, better for soul and body both. How is it that even good men have come to think so little of nature, as if to love her and seek her haunts and companionship were a waste of time? I have been astonished at the remarks sometimes made to me on my long jaunts in the woods, as if it were almost wicked to cast off the gravity of society, and wander like a child amid the beauty which God has spread out with such a lavish hand over the earth. Why, I should as soon think of feeling reproved for gazing on the midnight heavens, gorgeous with stars, and fearful with its mysterious floating worlds. I believe that every man degenerates without frequent communion with nature. It is one of the open books of God, and more replete with instructions than anything ever penned by man. A single tree standing alone, and waving all day long its green crown in the summer wind, is to me fuller of meaning and instruction than the crowded mart or gorgeously built town.

Burt.

A SCENE ON FORKED LAKE.

XIX.

LONG LAKE COLONY—A LOON—FORKED LAKE.

FORKED LAKE, August.

DEAR H——:

TAKING Mitchell along with me, we embarked on Monday in his birch bark canoe for Forked and Raquette Lakes. Paddling leisurely up Long Lake, I was struck with the desolate appearance of the settlement. Scarcely an improvement has been made since I was last here, while some clearings are left to go back to their original wildness. Disappointed purchasers, lured in by extravagant statements, have given up in despondency and left—the best people are all going away, and in a short time there will be nobody left but hunters. This wilderness will be encroached upon in time, though it will require years to give us so crowded a population as to force settlements into this desolate interior of the State.

But our light canoes soon left the last clearing; and curving round the shore, we shot into Raquette River, and entered the bosom of the forest. As we left the lake, I saw a northern diver some distance up the inlet, evidently anxious to get out once more into open space. These birds (about the size of a goose,) you know, cannot rise from the water except by a long effort, and against a strong damp wind; and depend for safety entirely on diving, and swimming. At the approach of danger, they go under like a duck, and when you next see them, they are perhaps sixty rods distant, and beyond the reach of your bullet. If cornered in a small pond, they will sit and watch your motions with a keenness and certainty that is wonderful, and dodge the flash of a percussion-lock gun all day long. The moment they see the blaze from the muzzle they dive, and the bullet, if well aimed, will strike exactly where they sat. I have shot at them again and again, with a dead rest, and those watching, would see the ball each time, strike in the hollow made by the wake of the water above the creature's back. There is no killing them except by firing at them when they are not expecting it, and then their head and neck are the only vulnerable points. They sit so deep in the water, and the quills on their backs are so hard and compact that a ball seems to make no impression on them. At least, I have never seen one killed by being shot through the body. Such are the means of self-preservation possessed by this curious bird, whose wild, shrill, and lonely cry, on the lake at midnight, is one of the most melancholy sounds I ever heard in the forest.

This diver, of which I was just now speaking, I wished very much to kill, in order to carry his skin to New York with me; and so, after firing at him in vain, I asked Mitchell if we could not both of us together manage to take him. He told me to land him where the channel was narrow that entered Long Lake, and paddle along towards where the fellow was sitting, and drive him out. As I approached the bird, he dived. Knowing that he would make straight fo the lake, I watched the whole line of his progress with the utmost care: but though my range took in nearly a third of a mile, I never saw him again. After a while I heard the crack of a rifle around the bend of the shore; and hastening thither, I found Mitchell loading his gun. He said the rascal just raised his head above water for a single second, opposite where he stood, and he of course missed him. The frightened bird did not appear again till it rose far out in the lake.

I mention this circumstance merely to show the habits of this, to me, most singular bird of our northern waters. I forgot to say that although it cannot rise from the water except with great difficulty, and never attempts it to escape danger, neither can it walk on the shore. Diving is about the only gift it possesses, which it uses, I must say, with great ability and success.

Paddling up Raquette river, we at length came to Buttermilk Falls, around which we were compelled to carry our canoes. So in another place we were compelled to carry them two miles, around rapids, through the woods. Nothing can be more comical than to stand and see a party thus passing through the forest. First a yoke is placed across the guide's neck, on which the boat is balanced bottom side up, covering the poor fellow down to the shoulders, and sticking out fore and aft over the biped below in such a way as to make him appear half human, half-supernatural, or, at least, entirely *un*-natural. But it was no joke to me to carry my part of the freight. Two rifles, one overcoat, one tea-pot, one lantern, one basin, and a piece of pork, were my portion. Sometimes I had a change—namely, two oars and a paddle, balanced by a tin pail in place of a rifle. Thus equipped, I would press on for a while, and then stop to see the procession—each poor fellow staggering under the weight he bore, while in the long intervals appeared the two inverted boats, walking through the woods on two human legs in the most surprising manner imaginable. Though tired and fagged out, I could not refrain from frequent outbursts of laughter, that made the forest ring again. But there was no other way of getting along, and each one had to become a beast of burden.

It was a relief to launch again, and when at last we struck the river just after it leaves Forked Lake, and gazed on the beautiful sheet of water that was rolling and sparkling in the sunlight ahead, an involuntary shout burst from the party. A flock of wild ducks, scared at the sound, made the water foam as they rose at our feet and sped away. Stemming the rapid stream with our light prows, we were soon afloat on the bosom of the lake. The wind was blowing directly in our teeth, making the miniature waves leap and dance around us as if welcoming us to their home—a white gull rose from a rock at our side—a fish hawk screamed around her huge nest on a lofty pine-tree on the shore, as she wheeled and circled above her offspring—a raven croaked overhead—the cry of loons arose in the distance—and all was wild yet beautiful. The sun was stooping to the western mountains, whose sea of summits were calmly sleeping against the golden heavens: the cool breeze stirred a world of foliage on our right—green islands, beautiful as Elysian fields, rose out of the water as we advanced; the sparkling waves rolled as merrily under as bright a sky as ever bent over the earth, and for a moment I seemed to have been transported into a new world. I never was more struck by a scene in my life: its utter wildness, spread out there where the axe of civilization has never struck a blow—the evening—the sunset—the deep purple of the mountains—the silence and solitude of the shores, and the cry of birds in the distance, combined to render it one of enchantment to me. My feelings were more excited, perhaps, by the consciousness that we were without any definite object before us—no place of rest, but sailing along looking out for some good point of land on which to pitch our camp.

Mitchell made no replies to our inquiries, but kept paddling along among the lily pads until he reached a point near the Raquette river and mooring our boats to the shore, began to prepare for the night.

Yours truly.

XX.

SHOOTING A DEER—MODERN SENTIMENTALISTS—THE INFLUENCE OF NATURE.

FORKED LAKE, Aug.

AFTER we had pitched (not our tent, but) our shanty, we began to cast about for supper. I told Mitchell I could not think of eating a piece of salt pork, and we must get some trout. So rigging our lines upon poles we cut on the shores of the lake, and taking our rifles with us, we jumped into our bark canoe, and pushed for some rapids in the Raquette River, where it entered Forked Lake. As we were paddling carefully along the edge of a marsh that put out from the main land, Mitchell, who was at the stern, suddenly exclaimed, "Hist!—I see the head of deer coming down to feed." I sometimes thought he could *smell* a deer, for he would often say he saw one before both his ears had fairly emerged from the bushes. "Shoot him," he said to me. "I can't," I replied; "I am too tired: shoot him yourself." So stooping my head to let the bullet pass over me, I watched him as he took aim; and it was a sight worth seeing. The careless, indolent manner so natural to him had disappeared as if by magic, and he stood up in the stern of the boat as straight as his own rifle, while his dark eye glanced like an eagle's. Every nerve in him seemed to have been suddenly touched by an electric spark—and as he now stooped to elude the watchfulness of the deer, and now again stood erect, with his rifle raised to his shoulder, he was one of the most picturesque objects I ever saw. The timorous doe was feeding on the marsh, and ever and anon lifted her head as if she scented danger in the air. Then Mitchell would drop like a flash, and gently rise again as the deer returned to her feed. She was about twenty rods off, and now stood fairly exposed amid the grass. It was a long shot for arm's length, and a tottlish boat to stand in, but he resolved to try it. Slowly bringing his rifle to his face, he stood for a moment as motionless as a pillar of marble, while his gun seemed suddenly to have frozen in its place, so still and steady did it lie in his bronze hand. A flash—a quick sharp report, and the noble deer bounded several feet into the air, then wheeled and sprang into the forest. He had shot directly over my head, and the mad bound of the animal told too well that the unerring bullet had struck near the life. Rowing hastily to the spot, we could find no traces of blood, but Mitchell, with his eye bent on the ground, paced backward and forward without saying a word. At length he stopped and peering down amid the long grass, said, "Here is blood." How he discovered it is a perfect mystery to me, for the grass was a foot long and very thick, while the drop which had fallen on the roots of a single blade, I never should have noticed, and if I had, have considered it a mere discoloration of the leaf, fac similies of which occurred at every step. The keen hawk eye of the Indian hunter, however, could not be deceived, and he simply remarked, "She is hit deep, or she would have bled more," and struck on the trail. But this baffled even, for the marsh was covered with deer tracks, while the bushes into whicl the wounded one had sprung were a perfect matting of laurels and low shrubs. There was no more blood to be found, and we were completely at fault in our search.

At length, tired and disappointed, I returned to the boat; and stood waiting the return of Mitchell, when the sharp crack of his rifle again rang through the forest, followed soon after by a shrill whistle. I knew then that a deer had fallen, and hastened to the spot. There lay the beautiful creature stretched on the moss, with the life-blood welling from her throat, and over the body, watching, stood Mitchell, leaning on his rifle. Unable to find the trail, he had made a shrewd guess as to the course the animal had taken, and making a circuit, finally came upon her, lain down to die. At his approach she sprang to her feet, ran a few rods, fell again exhausted, when his deadly aim planted a bullet directly back of her ear, and her career was ended.

Satisfied with our game, we gave up the fishing, and dragging the body to the boat, put back to our camp. The rest of our company stood on the shore waiting our return, for they had heard the shots, and were expecting the spoils. Some, no doubt, will think this very cruel, and congratulate themselves on their kinder natures. I have seen such people, and heard them expend whole sentences of sentimentality upon the hard-heartedness that could take the life of so innocent a creature, who very coolly wrung the necks of chickens every night for their breakfast, and devoured with great gusto the shoulder of a lamb for dinner. They slay without remorse the most harmless, trusting creatures that haunt their meadows, or sport upon their lawns and take food from their hands, and yet are shocked at the idea of killing a deer or shooting a wild pigeon. *They* kill God's creatures, not from necessity, but to gratify their palates and minister to their luxurious tastes. But if any one supposes we shot this noble doe for sport, he must have a very vague idea of the toils we had endured that day, or of our keen appetites. A man of great sentimentality might eat boiled eggs and toast with his coffee for breakfast, rather than sanction the death of an animal by partaking of flesh. I say he *might* do it, though I have never seen an instance of such great self-denial; but I doubt whether, if he were a day's journey from a human habitation, hungry and tired, with the prospect of nothing but a piece of salt pork, toasted on the end of a stick for supper and breakfast, he would hesitate to eat a venison steak.

But I like to have forgot—the pork, too, was the flesh of an animal, and it would be difficult to convince a hog that he had not as good a right to life as a deer. At all events, we enjoyed the venison, though perhaps the sentimentalist might say we were punished in the end, for it made us all outrageously sick. We either cooked it too soon, (for in twenty minutes from the time the deer fell, a part of her was roasting;) or we ate it too rare, (for we were too hungry to wait till it was perfectly done;) or we ate too much, (for we were hungry as famished wolves;) or probably did all three things together, which quite upset me.

But after the things (i. e. the chips) were cleared away, I stretched myself on the ground under a tree whose dark trunk shone in the light of the cheerful fire, and began to muse on the day that had past. How is it that a scene of quiet beauty makes so much deeper an impression than a startling one? The glorious sunset I had witnessed on that sweet lake—the curving and forest-mantled shores—the green islands—the mellow mountains, all combined to make a scene of surpassing loveliness: and now as I lay and watched the stars coming out one after another, and twinkling down on me through the tree-tops, all that beauty came back on me with strange power. The gloomy gorge and savage precipice, or the sudden storm, seem to excite the surface only of one's feelings, while the sweet vale, with its cottages and herds and evening bells, blends itself in with our very thoughts and emotions, forming a part of our after existence. Such a scene sinks away into the heart like a gentle rain into the earth, while a rougher, nay, sublimer one, comes and goes like a sudden shower. I do not know how it is that the gentler influence should be the deeper and more lasting, but so it is. The still small voice of nature is more impressive than her loudest thunder. Of all the scenery in the Alps, and there is no grander on the earth, nothing is so plainly daguerreotyped on my heart as two or three lovely valleys I saw. Those heaven-piercing summits, and precipices of ice, and terrific gorges, and fearful passes, are like grand but indistinct visions on my memory, while those vales, with their carpets of greensward, and murmuring rivulets, and perfect repose, have become a part of my life. In moments of high excitement or turbulent grief they rise before me with their gentle aspect and quiet beauty, hushing the storm into repose, and subduing the spirit like a sensible presence.

But Mitchell has arisen from his couch of leaves, where he has been reclining silent and thoughtful as his race, and is looking up to the sky and out upon the lake, and I know something is afoot.

Yours truly.

XXI.

FLOATING DEER—A NIGHT EXCURSION—MORNING IN THE WOODS.

FORKED LAKE, Aug.

DEAR H——:

As I stated in my last, Mitchell looked up to the sky, and out upon the lake a moment, and then, in that quiet way so characteristic of his race, said, "If you want to go after a deer it is time we started." It took but five minutes to load my rifle, put on my overcoat, and announce myself ready. Lifting our bark canoe softly from the rocks, we launched it on the still water, and stepping carefully in, pushed off. Previously, however, Mitchell requested me to try one of my matches, to see if the damp had affected them.

You know that deer-floating amid backwoodsmen is very different from deer-stalking in Scotland. In the warm, summer months, the deer come down from the mountains at night to feed on the marshes that line the shores of the lakes and rivers.* While they are thus feeding, if you pass along in a dark, still night, without making a noise, you can hear them, as they step about in the edge of the water, or snort as they scent approaching danger. The moment you become aware of the proximity of one, strike a light and fix it firmly in the bow of your boat, or in a lantern on your head, and advance cautiously. The deer, attracted by the flame, stops and gazes intently upon it. If he hears no sound he will not stir till you are close to him. At first you catch only the sight of his two eyes, burning like fire-balls in the gloom, but as you approach nearer, the light is thrown on his red flanks, and he stands revealed in all his beautiful proportions before you. The candle serves to distinguish the animal, and, at the same time, give you a clear view of the sights along your gun-barrel, and he must be a poor shot who misses at five rods' distance.

* Sportsmen may wonder at our killing deer in *midsummer*, but I would say that we never shot a sucking doe. Bucks never are better than in July, for the food is then so abundant they are extremely fat. We killed only one *doe* in all, and that was a *yearling*.

This night, the only good feeding spot for deer had been so trampled over by us, before dark, that they would not come out upon it, and we floated on for a a long time without hearing anything. I never before saw such an exhibition of the stealthy movements of an Indian. The lake was as still and smooth as a polished mirror, and our frail canoe floated over it as if impelled by an invisible hand. I knelt at the bow, with my rifle before me, while Mitchell sat in the stern as fixed as a statue, yet urging the boat on by some strange movement of the paddle, which I tried in vain to comprehend. He did not even make a ripple on the water, and I could tell we were moving only by marking the shadow of trees we crossed, or the stars we passed over. Though straining every nerve to catch a sound, I never once heard the stroke of his paddle. It was the most mysterious ride I ever took. We entered the mouth of a river, whose shores were black with the sombre fir trees, while ever and anon would come more clearly on the ear the roar of a distant waterfall. It was so dark I could make out nothing distinctly on shore, and the island-like tufts that here and there rose from the water—the little bays and rocky points we passed, assumed the most grotesque shapes to my fancy, till I had all the feelings of one suddenly transported to a fairy land. Now the silent boat would cross the shadow of a lofty pine tree, that lay dark and calm in the water below, and now sail over a bright constellation that sparkled in our path, while the scream of a far-off loon came ringing like a spirit's cry through the gloom. Oh, how bright lay the sky, with its sapphire floor beneath us, and how black was the fringe of shadow that encroached on its beauty, and yet added to it by contrast. The silent night around me—the strangeness of the place, and the far removal from human habitations, were enough in themselves; but the dim, impalpable objects on shore, just distinct enough to confuse the senses, added tenfold mystery to the scene. I seemed moving through a boundless world of shadows, with nothing clear and natural, but the bright constellations below me.

Thus we continued on for a mile, without a whisper or sign having passed between us. At length the canoe entered what seemed at first a deep bay, but soon changed to the mouth of a gloomy cavern. I leaned forward, striving in vain to make out the misshapen objects before me; but the more I looked, the more confused I grew; while to add to my bewilderment, suddenly the dim outlines I was struggling to make out, began to vanish as if melting away in the darkness. At first, I thought the whole had been a structure of mist, and was dissolving in my sight, but casting my eyes beneath me, I saw we were *receding* over the stars. Then I understood it all. Mitchell, without making a sound, had drawn the boat slowly backwards, causing the objects before me to fade thus strangely from my sight. He knew the ground perfectly well, and could enter every bay and inlet as accurately as in broad daylight.

Pursuing our way up the channel, I was at length startled by a low "hist!" The next moment I caught the tread of a deer on shore, when the light canoe shot along the surface till I could hear the low ripple of the water around the bow. "Light up!" said Mitchell in a whisper. As quietly as possible, I kindled a match, and lighting a candle, put it in a lantern made to fit the head like a hat, and clapping it in the place of my cap, cocked my rifle and leaned forward. The bright flame flared out upon the surrounding gloom, and all was hush as death. But as we advanced towards where the deer was standing, the boat suddenly struck the dry limbs of a spruce tree that had fallen in the water. Snap, snap, went the brittle twigs—one of them piercing our bark canoe. We backed out of the dilemma as quick as possible, but the sound had alarmed the deer, and I could hear his long bounds as he cleared the bank, and made off into the forest.

After cruising about a little while longer, we put back, and crossed the lake to a deep bay on the farther side. But the moon now began to show her disc over the fir trees, and our last remaining chance was to find a deer in the bay before the silver orb should climb the lofty pines that folded it in. But in this too we were disappointed, and the unclouded light now flooding lake and forest, we turned wearily towards our camp fire that was blazing cheerfully amid the trees on the farther shore. Just then a merry laugh came floating over the water from our companions there, breaking the silence which had enchained us, and for the first time we spoke. My limbs were almost paralyzed from having been kept so long in one position, and I was sick and weary. Still I would not have missed that mysterious boat-ride and the strange sensations it had awakened, to have been saved from thrice the inconvenience it had occasioned me. It was one of those new things in this stereotyped life of ours, imparting new experiences, and giving one as it were a deeper insight into his own soul.

At length we stretched ourselves upon the boughs, and were soon fast asleep. I awoke, however, about midnight, and found our fire reduced to a few embers, while the rain was coming down as if that were its sole business for the night. It is gloomy in the woods without a fire; and I never seem so companionless as when in the still midnight I awake and find nothing but the dark forest about me, cheered by no light. A bright, crackling flame seems like a living thing, keeping awake on purpose to watch over you.

Leaving my companions, whose heavy breathings told how profound were their slumbers, I sallied out in search of fuel. But there was nothing but green fir trees, which would not burn, to be found; and after striking my axe into several, and getting my lower extremities thoroughly wet, I returned, and lay down again and slept till morning. With the first dawn I was up, and taking the Indian's canoe, pushed off in search of a deer. The heavy fog lay in masses upon the water, and the damp morning was still and quiet as the night that had passed. I floated about till the sun rose over the mountains, turning that lake into a sheet of gold, and sending the mist in spiral wreaths skyward, and then slowly paddled my way back to our camp. As I was thus floating tranquilly along over the water, I heard far up the lake, where it lost itself in the mountains, two distinct and heavy reports like the discharge of fire-arms. Who could be in that solitude besides ourselves? was the first enquiry. I mentioned the circumstance when I reached the camp, and found that my companions, who had been busy in preparing breakfast, had also been startled by the sound. Mitchell, just then returned from an expedition after a fish-hawk, which he brought back with him, hearing our conjectures, very quietly remarked, they were not rifle shots. His quick ear never deceived him. "What, then, were they?" I enquired. "Trees," he replied. "But," said I, "there is not a breath of air this morning, while it blew very hard yesterday afternoon." "They always fall," he replied, "before a storm—it will storm to-morrow." There was something sad in thinking of those two trees thus falling all alone on a still and beautiful morning, foretelling a coming tempest. Sombre omens these, and mysterious, as becomes the untrodden forest.

Mitchell had shot an immense fish-hawk, breaking only the tip of his wing, so as to prevent him from flying. He brought him and set him down before the fire, when the fearless bird drew himself proudly up and steadily faced us down without attempting to run away. His savage eye betokened no fear, and when any one of us approached him, his leg would be lifted and his talons expanded ready to strike. I was never so struck with the boldness of a bird in my life. At length Mitchell took him and placed him on a rock by the edge of the lake, when, for a moment, he forgot his wound, and spreading his broad wings, leaped from his resting place. But the broken pinion refused to carry him heavenward, and he fell heavily into the water. I saw Mitchell bring his rifle to his shoulder, and the next moment a bullet crushed through the head of the poor creature, and its sufferings were over.

Such are the incidents cf a life in the woods, and thus do the days and nights pass—not without meaning or instruction. A man cannot move or look without thinking of God, for all that meets his eye is just as it left his mighty hand. The old forest as it nods to the passing wind speaks of him—the still mountain points towards his dwelling-place, and the calm lake reflects his sky of stars and sunshine. The glorious sunset and the blushing dawn—the gorgeous midnight and the noon-day splendor, mean more in these solitudes than in the crowded city. Indeed, they look different—they *are* different.

Yours truly

XXII.

FOREST MUSIC.

THE WOODS, August.

DEAR H——:

How often we speak of the *solitude* of the forest, meaning by that, the contrast its stillness presents to the hum and motion of busy life. When you first step from the crowded city into the centre of a vast wilderness, the absence of all the bustle and activity you have been accustomed to makes you at first believe there is no sound, no motion there. So a man accustomed for a long time to the surges of the ocean cannot at first hear the murmur of the rill. Yet these solitudes are full of sound, aye, of rare music, too. I do not mean the notes of birds, for they rarely sing in the darker, deeper portions of the forest. Even the robin, which in the fields cannot chirp and carol enough, and is so tame that a tyro can shoot him, ceases his song the moment he enters the forest, and flits silently from one lofty branch to another, as if in constant fear of a secret enemy. If you want to listen to the music of birds, go to some field that borders on the woods, and there, before sunrise of a summer morning, you will hear such an orchestra as never before greeted your ears. There are no dying cadences and rapturous bursts and prolonged swells, but one continuous strain of joy. Yet there is every variety of tone, from the clear, round note of the robin, to the shrill piping of the sparrow. No time is kept, and no scale is followed—each is striving to outwarble the other, and yet there seems the most perfect accord. No jar is made by all the conflicting instruments—the whole heavens are full of voices tuned to a different key—each pausing or breaking in as it suits its mood—and yet the harmony remains the same. It is *unwritten* music such as nature furnishes—filling the soul with a delight and joy it never before experienced.

But this is found only in the fields—our great forests are too sombre and shadowy for such glees. Still you find music there. There is a certain kind occurring only at intervals, which chills the heart like a dead-march, and is fearful as the echo of bursting billows along the arches of a cavern. The shrill scream of a panther in the midst of an impenetrable swamp, rising in the intervals of thunder claps—the long, discordant howl of a herd of wolves at midnight, slowly traveling along the slope of a high mountain, you may call strange music; yet there are certain chords in the heart of man, that quiver to it, especially when he feels there is no cause of alarm. The lowing of a moose, echoing miles away in the gorges —the solitary cry of the loon in some deep bay—the solemn hoot of the owl, the only lullaby that cradles you to sleep, all have their charms, and stir you at times like the blast of a bugle. So the scream of the eagle, and cry of the fish-hawk, as they sweep in measured circles over the still bosom of a lake after their prey, or the low, half suppressed croak of the raven—his black form like some messenger of death, slowly swinging from one mountain to another—are sights and sounds that arrest and chain you. Yet these are not all—the ear grows sensitive when you feel that everything about you treads stealthily; and the slightest noise will sometimes startle you like the unexpected crack of a rifle.

After watching for a long time for deer on the banks of some still stream, almost motionless myself, the unexpected spring of a trout to the surface has sent the blood to my temples as suddenly as though it had been the leap of a panther.

By living in the woods, your sense of hearing becomes so acute that the wilderness never seems silent. It is said that a nice and practised ear can hear at night, in the full vigor of spring, the low sound of growing, bursting vegetation, and in the winter, the shooting of crystals, "like moon-beams splintering along the ground." So in the forest, there is a faint and indistinct hum about you, as if the spreading and bursting of the buds and barks of trees, the stretching out of the roots into the earth, and the slow and affectionate interlacing of branches and kiss of leaves, were all perceptible to the ear. The passage of the scarcely moving air over the unseen tree tops, the motion it gives to the trunk—too slight to be detected by the eye—the dropping of an imperfect leaf; all combine to produce a monotonous sound, which lulls you into a feeling half melancholy and half pleasing. You may, on a still summer afternoon, recline for hours on some gentle slope, and listen without weariness to this low, perpetual chant of nature. Sometimes the hollow tap of the woodpecker, or the loud, babbling voice of the streamlet, rushing under arches of evergreens, gives animation to the song. If you are on the borders of a lake, the clear and limpid sound of the ripples, as they hasten to lay their lips on the smooth pebbles, blend in with the anthem, till the soul sinks into reveries it dare not speak aloud.

But there is one kind of forest music I love best of all—it is the sound of wind amid the trees. I have lain here by the hour, on some fresh afternoon, when the brisk west wind swept by in gusts, and listened to it. All is comparatively still, when, far away, you catch a faint murmur, like the dying tone of an organ with its stops closed—gradually swelling into clearer distinctness and fuller volume, as if gathering strength for some fearful exhibition of its power; until, at length, it rushes like a sudden sea overhead, and everything sways and tosses about you. For a moment an invisible spirit seems to be near—the fresh leaves rustle and talk to each other—the pines and cedars whisper ominous tidings, and then the retiring swell subsides in the distance, and silence again slowly settles on the forest. A short interval only elapses when the murmur, the swell, the rush, and the retreat, are repeated. If you abandon yourself entirely to the influence, you soon are lost in strange illusions. I have lain and listened to the wind moving thus among the branches, until I fancied every gust a troop of spirits, whose tread over the bending tops I caught afar, and whose rapid approach I could distinctly measure. My heart would throb and pulses bound, as the invisible squadrons drew near, till as their sounding chariots of air swept swiftly overhead, I ceased listening, and turned *to look.* Thus troop after troop, they came and went on their mysterious mission—waking the solitude into sudden life, as they passed, and filling it with glorious melody.

From such a state of reverie I was once aroused by my Indian guide quietly saying, "It blows most too hard to fish to-night." Oh, yes, it blows too hard: ye splendid train of spirits treading the soft and velvet bosom of the boundless forest, and with ten times ten thousand branches and twigs and leaves for harp strings, discoursing sweet music, you march altogether too heavily, and sing too loudly for *good fishing*. Good Mitchell, you are right; those spirits have kicked the lake all into a bubble. We both have been listening to this wind, but with how different ears—you as a practical man, and I as a dreamer. I am half a mind to tell you what I have been thinking about, just to see your black eyes stare. But it is of no use; we must take a little salt pork instead of trout for supper to-night—thanks to the "forest music."

Yours truly.

Hill. Burt.

VIEW ON RAQUETTE LAKE.

Hill. Burt.

VIEW ON RAQUETTE LAKE.

XXIII.

RAQUETTE LAKE—NUMBER OF ITS TROUT—A HUNTER'S LOVE FOR AN EAGLE—FIERCE STRUGGLE BETWEEN AN EAGLE AND A SALMON.

RAQUETTE LAKE, August.

DEAR H——:

IT is only about a mile and a half from Crotched or Forked to Raquette Lake. For about three quarters of a mile up the inlet, where Mitchell shot the deer the first night we arrived at Forked Lake, it is fair rowing to the falls—then for a half a mile you are compelled to shoulder your boats. But at length the beautiful sheet of Raquette Lake opens on the view, shining like an opal amid an interminable mass of green. Stretching away for nearly thirteen miles, it lies embosomed in the unshorn shores, and reflecting in its pellucid depths the clouds, as they float over the heavens which seem immeasurably high here in this clear atmosphere—and presents one of the most beautiful scenes the eye ever rested upon. When, however, the mountain storm sweeps over its breast, and the confined thunder breaks and bursts upon it, it looks like any thing but a gentle being.

It is the largest body of water in this wild region, and with a shore as irregular as it could well be made. Though only thirteen miles long and six broad, it has a coast of *fifty miles in extent.* With its long, wooded points and promontories and deep bays, it would look, to a man placed above it, like a huge scollop. This waving outline completely deceives one, in sailing over it, as to the extent and direction of the main body of water. As you round one point, the lake seems to take a turn, for it goes miles away, piercing the very heart of the distant forest. But, by the time a second point is weathered, a broad and beautiful surface is seen spreading in another direction. Thus there is a constant succession of new views—in fact, as you slowly float along, you seem to behold a dozen different lakes, each rivalling the other in picturesque beauty. It has three large inlets, one of which comes from the Eckford [illegible]or, as the hunters call them, Blue Mountain and Tallow Lakes, pouring a stream of crystal into its bosom. The south inlet is a river of such magnitude that it can be navigated for eight miles by a boat of a ton's burthen. The third is Brown's inlet, of almost half the size of the former.

Imagine this broad expanse of water in the midst of a vast wilderness, dotted with islands, with deep bays fringed with green—bold slopes reaching to the clouds, clothed with green—distant mountains enfolding mountains, all waving with the same rich verdure—blue peaks dreaming far away, and far up in the heavens, and not a sign of vegetation—not a boat to break the solitude, and you will have some idea of the sights that meet you at every turn, charming the soul into pleasure.

Thus rowing along, with no living thing but the wild bird, and wilder deer, which has come down from the mountains to drink, and raises his head as the sound of your voice is borne to his ear, to interrupt the Sabbath quietness around, you at length come in sight of "Indian Point," so called because there was once an Indian settlement upon it. Now two huts are standing there, looking like oases in the desert, occupied by two men, who dwell thus shut out from civilized life.

These two cabins are the only ones on this whole fifty miles of coast,* and the two hunters that occupy them the only inhabitants that are or have been on the shore for the last nine years. Without a wife or child they have lived here winter and summer, as ignorant of what is going on in the great world without, and as indifferent to it as the savage of the Rocky Mountains. One of them was once a wealthy manufacturer; but overtaken by successive misfortunes, he at length fled to the wilderness, where he has ever since lived. There is also a rumor, of some love adventure—of blasted affections followed by morbid melancholy, which is probably "ower true"—being the cause of this strange self-exile.

However that may be, here he lives, and here he is likely to live and be buried. These two Robinson Crusoes have cleared about ten acres of land, on which they raise such vegetables as they need, while the fishing line and rifle supplies them with meat. An easy life is theirs—no taxes to pay—no purchases to

* There are others now.

make—and during most of the year, fish and deer and moose ready to come almost at their call.

This beautiful lake is thronged with salmon and speckled trout. Talk about Pisico Lake and Lake Pleasant, and other border waters, where fishing has become a business. Come here, if you wish to see the treasures the wilderness encloses. The most beautiful and savory trout that ever swam are found in such quantities that you can take them without even a fly, or bait of any description. Look at that inlet—there sits my friend B——n with a pole and line big enough to play a sturgeon with, and nothing but a piece of white paper on his coarse hook. He is skipping it, or as the fishermen call it, "skittering" it over the water, and there rises a two pounder, and there a three pounder, and a one pounder by his side—heigh ho, a full dozen of them, with their speckled, gleaming sides and wild eyes, are making the water foam about it. The hungry, unsophisticated fellows have never yet learned that there is such a thing as a hook, and dart fiercely at every object that tempts their appetite, without fear of being caught. You can sit here of a fine day, and with bait take out these speckled trout till your arms ache with lifting them. No sooner does the worm, or piece of venison, sink in the water than they crowd round it in swarms.

The salmon trout are noble fellows—these two hunters say they have caught them weighing over *thirty pounds.*

I have often been struck with the singular attachment hunters sometimes have for some bird or animal, while all the rest of the species they pursue with deadly hostility.

About five hundred yards from Beach's hut, stands a lofty pine tree, on which a grey eagle has built its nest annually during the nine years he has lived on the shores of the Raquette. The Indian who dwelt there before him, says that the same pair of birds made their nest on that tree for ten years previous—making in all, nineteen years they have occupied the same spot, and built on the same branch. It is possible, however, that the young may have taken the place of their parents. At all events, Beach believes them to be the same old dwellers, and hence regards them as squatters like himself, and entitled to equal privileges. From his cabin door he can see them in sunshine and storm—quietly perched on the tall pine, or wildly cradled as the mighty fabric bends and sways to the blast. He has become attached to them, and hence requests every one who visits him not to touch them. I verily believe he would like to shoot the man who should harm one of their feathers. They are his companions in that solitude—proud occupants of the same wild home, and hence bound together by a link it would be hard to define, and yet which is strong as steel. If that pine tree should fall, and those eagles move away to some other lake, he would feel as if he had lost a friend, and the solitude become doubly lonely.

Thus it is—you cannot by any education or experience, drive all the poetry out of a man—it lingers there still, and blazes up unexpectedly—revealing the human heart with all the sympathies, attachments, and tenderness that belong to it.

He, however, one day came near losing his bold eagle. He was lying at anchor, fishing, when he saw his favorite bird high up in heaven, slowly sweeping round and round in a huge circle, evidently awaiting the approach of a fish to the surface. For an hour or more, he thus sailed with motionless wings above the water, when all at once he stopped and hovered a moment, with an excited gesture—then rapid as a flash of light, and with a rush of his broad pinions, like the passage of a sudden gust of wind, came to the still bosom of the lake. He had seen a huge salmon trout swimming near the surface—and plunging from his high watch-tower, drove his talons deep in his victim's back. So rapid and strong was his swoop that he buried himself out of sight when he struck, but the next moment he emerged into view, and flapping his wings, endeavored to rise with his prey. But this time he had miscalculated his strength—in vain he struggled nobly to lift the salmon from the water. The frightened and bleeding fish made a sudden dive, and took eagle and all out of sight, and was gone a quarter of a minute. Again they arose to the surface, and the strong bird spread his broad, dripping pinions, and gathering force with his rapid blows, raised the salmon half out of water. The weight, however, was too great for him, and he sank again to the surface, beating the water into foam about him. The salmon then made another dive, and they both went under, leaving only a few bubbles to tell where they had gone down. This time they were absent a full half minute, and Beach said he thought it was all over with his bird. He soon, however, reappeared with his talons still buried in the flesh of his foe, and again made a desperate effort to rise. All this time the fish was shooting like an arrow through the lake, carrying his relentless foe on his back. He could not keep the eagle down, nor the bird carry him up—and so now beneath, and now upon the surface, they struggled on, presenting one of the most singular yet exciting spectacles that can be imagined. It was fearful to witness the blows of the eagle as he lashed the lake with his wings into spray, and made the shores echo with the report. At last, the bird thinking, as they say west, that he had "waked up the wrong passenger," gave it up; and loosening his clutch, soared heavily and slowly away to his lofty pine tree, where he sat for a long time sullen and sulky—the picture of disappointed ambition. So might a wounded and baffled lion lie down in his lair and brood over his defeat. Beach said that he could easily have captured them, but he thought he would see the fight out. When, however, they both staid under a half minute or more, he concluded he should never see his eagle again. Whether the latter in his rage was bent on capturing his prize, and would retain his hold though at the hazard of his life, or whether in his terrible swoop he had struck his crooked talons so deep in the back of the salmon, he could not extricate himself, the hunter said he could not tell. The latter, however, was doubtless the truth, and he would have been glad to have let go, long before he did. The old fellow probably spent the afternoon in studying avoirdupois weight, and ever after tried his tackle on smaller fish. As for the poor salmon, if he survived the severe laceration, he doubtless never fully understood the operation he had gone through.

XXIV.

DESCRIPTION OF RAQUETTE LAKE—ABUNDANCE OF ITS FISH—LAKE ELDON—ITS QUEER DISCOVERY—A MAN WHIPPED BY AN EAGLE—A HUNTER WITHOUT FEET.

The Woods, August.

Dear H——:

I designed to give you a lengthy description of Raquette Lake, which surpasses all the others in the beauty of its scenery, and can hardly be matched in the wide world. I was the more anxious to do this, because its sloping shores and fertile land make it the most desirable portion of this whole region for settlers. The Adirondack chain terminates here in the isolated peak of Mount Emmons, and the land sinks into an elevated plateau, furnishing many inducements to the emigrant. In place of this, however, I give you an extract from an interesting letter which I received from a gentleman who has spent months around the Raquette.

"There are, perhaps, but few sections in our country, where the *amateur* of the beauties of nature, and the lover of sport, can better enjoy a few days of retreat from the thronged city and the cares of business, than at Raquette Lake. Here he feels liberated from the restraints of organized society, and meets the rude yet agreeable change, produced by an escape from the formalities of the world—indeed, he enters upon the enjoyment of that pure and artless freedom which the *society of nature* alone can impart. As a striking proof of the effect of this change, one can scarcely turn his attention from the objects around him, to the calculations of business, or the schemes of selfishness and pride—and I venture to say, if the mines of California were planted upon the shores of this beautiful lake, the miser even, would forsake his sordid labor, till he had viewed and *re-viewed* the enchanting landscape around him, while the man of taste would be absorbed as it were, in the midst of a new creation; and not an hour would pass, but what he would find something to admire, or amuse him.

"The natural scenery of the Raquette is, however,

not so much distinguished for its *sublimity* as its *beauty*. Unlike the lakes of Switzerland, those of northern New York, making an extensive chain from the Saranac waters to the Moose River Lakes, are not surrounded by summits of perpetual snow, nor by naked rocks towering one above another in fragmentary peaks and disordered masses, but, for the most part, especially the south-western, are surrounded by gently-receding shores, swelling into moderate ridges, and bounding the view with a clear and beautiful outline of green hills—with here and there a conical mountain-top elevated in the distance. Nor do we, about the Raquette, discover any Alpine glaciers glittering in the sun, or huge masses of ice thundering down from their heights to the valleys below, but the country is made up of a broad *plateau*, elegantly varied upon its surface, and clothed by a rich and luxurious forest, and excelling all the others in the beauty of its situation, as well as in the fertility of its soil.

"As we take a more particular view of this lake, and the objects of interest in its immediate vicinity, we are at first struck with the crystal purity of its waters, and the irregularity of its form. Its waters are so clear, that objects on a bright, sunny day, can be seen to the depth of *thirty or forty feet*—the angler often finds himself in a state of suspense, between hope and fear, as he looks into the depths of the lake, and sees his speckled majesty darting about the hook, artfully trying the bait.

The irregular form of the lake also, when the whole from some eminence is brought under the eye of the spectator, presents an interesting feature in the prospect. It is wholly embraced within an area of seven miles square, and yet it is so indented with deep bays, projecting points, and headlands, that it presents a shore of about fifty miles in extent, varying to every point of the compass, and marking the outlines of the lake, with a continuous round of graceful curves and angles; all of which are highly embellished by clusters of tall pines that stand upon the points, and skirt the shores, flinging their darkening shadows upon the water—while the thick wood and level surface, that fall back for some distance from the lake, gives a mellow aspect to the whole, and a highly satisfying indication of the character of the adjacent lands. But the islands that dot the lake with their dark, green forms, in lively contrast with the silvery surface of the waters that embrace them, are the most interesting objects connected with this landscape. From fifteen to twenty in number, they vary in size and form, from mere islets that cluster together in fantastic groups, to those of sufficient size for ordinary farms. Ospray Island, lying across the bay, one mile south of Beach and Woods, and half a mile west of Jos. Woods on Ospray Point, contains about thirty acres. This island derived its name from the ospray, that yearly builds her nest and rears her young thereon. Her nest is a prominent object in the view, being some three feet in diameter, and planted upon the top of the highest of a cluster of stately pines; and is so strongly interwoven with boughs and grass, as to resist the wind and storm. The sportsman delights to gaze upon this bird of solitude, as she returns from her excursions up the lake in quest of food, bearing the struggling trout in her talons, while her unfledged offspring, standing upon the verge of their aerial house, with untutored voices and fluttering wings, welcome her return. None disturb her domicile, or question her right to protection.

"Woods' Island, containing about three hundred

acres, lies in the southerly section of the lake. It has a level surface, fine dry soil, shaded with a clean and tasteful forest of beech and maple. In a warm summer's day, a ramble over this island, enjoying its shady groves, its gentle breezes from the lake, and its charming scenery, is truly delightful. Off its eastern extremity is a group of four islands, of nearly equal size, rising up out of the water, and studding the lake with their high conical forms, and their steep yet graceful shores. To the south the eye ranges along the blue surface of South Bay, until it rests upon the white sand beach that encircles its extremity; marking a line of separation between the land and the water, as white as a line of snow. This bay, moreover, is the favorite place of resort for the sportsman. Here the stately buck, after trying his speed with the hound, is wont to seek his safety by plunging into the water—unconscious that there is a worse enemy at hand, than the brute that hangs upon his track.

"Let the spectator overlook a scene like this, and at the same time bring within the scope of his vision the whole southern section of the lake, with its islands, indented shores, and conterminous forests, and a richer and more picturesque view can scarcely be imagined. Add to this the sullen stillness of the wilderness, where nature, unmarred by the hand of man, dwells in her primeval glory—her music the pealing thunder—the eagle's shrill voice—the wild notes of the loon—and the sound of the gentle breeze as it ruffles the surface of the lake—and no man of sensibility can escape the enchantment.

"The inlets of the lake form another interesting feature connected with its scenery. These, for the first few miles from the lake, move sluggishly along the valleys, through which they pass with singular tortuous windings, and of sufficient depth to float boats of large size. In the warm summer months, these inlets become the place of resort for the trout, where they are often taken with the hook in great numbers. They collect in schools around the cold springs that make into the inlets, and if approached with care and skill may be taken out, so eager are they for the bait, to the last, in the school. They will even dash at the hook as it approaches the surface of the water, and as the pole from time to time bends under the weight of its load, the skillful angler will deliberately bring his unwary captive to the shore. The salmon, or lake trout, however, seeks his summer retreat in the depths of the lake. These are usually found in its northern section, and are taken from a boat, with a long line let deep into the water. This is a more sober business, and often taxes the patience of the angler, before he feels the cautious bite—but if he is so fortunate as to fix his bearded hook in the jaws of his victim, he swells with pride and glories in his victory, as he plies the reel, or tugs at the line, and with hand over hand draws the ponderous fish into the boat. The largest trout of this description, known to have been taken in the lake, weighed *forty-five pounds*. Such a prize ought to satisfy the reasonable ambition of any sportsman.

"The Marion River is the largest inlet of the lake. It comes in from the east, and forms the connecting link between the Raquette and the Eckford Lakes. The valley embracing this stream and the last mentioned lakes, extends due east from the Raquette some twenty miles, and terminates at the base of Mount Emmons, which flings up its round head and giant form far above the blue range of hills that stretch on to the southeast. Mount Emmons is the most westerly of that group of high mountains that occupy the section of country between the Eckford Lakes and Lake Champlain; and overlooking the valley of the Raquette, forms the most prominent object in view towards the east. South and West inlets are also navigable streams, but more tortuous, if possible, in their course, than the Marion River. The boatman in passing up the west inlet, rows four miles to gain two in distance; he then arrives at the portage between the Raquette and Moose River waters.

"Nearly opposite Indian Point, connected with the Raquette by a small inlet only ten feet wide and four rods in length, there is a beautiful little lake, about one mile long and half a mile wide, of oval form, concealed in a rich, dark forest, where the pine, spruce, and hemlock, are gracefully intermixed with deciduous trees. This lovely retreat, called Lake Eldon, is protected from the winds in every direction, and affords a calm and delightful resort.

"Eagle Lake, which is an object of interest and curiosity, lies about three miles due south from the mouth of West Inlet, and two miles east of Eighth Lake. It is of small dimensions, not varying essentially from eighty chains in length and forty in breadth. This lake was discovered under circumstances somewhat amusing; and in a manner that presented its features in a bold and impressive aspect. Two gentlemen with their packs on their backs, left the east shore of Eighth Lake, in search of a lake discovered by Prof. Emmons, lying in that vicinity; but, as afterwards appeared, to the south of the one in question. After tugging some four or five hours, and surmounting several high ridges, crossing valleys, climbing over wind-falls, and tearing their way through the thick under-brush, they came to the summit of a still higher ridge, covered with thick spruces, so dense and dark, as to obstruct the view in every direction. Here they seated themselves upon a log to rest, and while calculating upon the probable proximity to the object of their search, they were startled by the cracking of the dry brush, under the footsteps of some heavy animal. They had left their trusty rifle behind them to lighten their burden, and their only means of defence consisted in an antiquated pistol, a family relic, that had seen much service, but which in this age of revolvers and improvements was, to say the least, of doubtful character. They, however, placed themselves in a posture of defence—

the redoubtable knight of the pistol, holding on to his anchorage on the log; while his defenceless companion veered round upon his stern, and took up his position *squat*, in the rear—this last movement having doubtless been made, not so much with a view to personal protection, as to form a *corps de reserve*, to fall upon the foe in the heat of the conflict. The heavy footsteps of the beast drew near, but the thicket still concealed him from their view. This suspense, however, did not continue long; for in due time, old Bruin presented his black visage, raised himself erect upon his haunches, skinned his teeth, uttered his hideous growl, and viewed the strangers with his keen, black eye. After exchanging glances for a short time, however, Bruin came to the conclusion "that discretion was the better part of valor," and with manifest symptoms of alarm, turned and fled, with the bullet from old '76 whistling through the thicket, in pursuit. Thus ended the fright and the bloodless contest, probably to the entire satisfaction of both parties concerned. But this adventure was followed by another, if not so dangerous, yet somewhat more amusing—which gave the name to the lake in question. Our travelers having been relieved from their unwelcome visitor, concluded, before they proceeded on with their journey, to take an observation from the high grounds where they were, with a view to examine the country to the south and east, and discover, if possible, the position of the lake, which was the object of their search. To accomplish this purpose, the knight of the pistol volunteered his services to climb a tall spruce that stood near by; and accordingly flung aside his pack, pulled off his boots, and depositing them *with his armor*, at the foot of the tree, commenced the ascent. After climbing some fifty or sixty feet, his ears were suddenly pierced by the screams of a huge eagle, and his face at the same time brushed by her wings, and torn by her claws. As the enraged bird passed round her airy circuit, repeating her sharp and threatening notes, the eye of the adventurer fell upon a deep, black lake below him, and he for the first time discovered that the tree he had ascended stood upon the brink of a precipice of fearful height, overhanging the dark abyss where the jealous bird of liberty had planted her nest, and secured her young. By this time the gathering foe had again made her circle, and coming like an arrow through the air, pounced upon his head, and striking her talons through his cap and wig, tore them from his naked scalp, and hurled them to the ground. Not exactly a back *out*, but a back *down*, was the immediate result—and the vanquished knight, as he landed upon *'erra firma*, audibly thanked his stars, and remarked to his companion, that his satisfaction was unbounded; seeing that the matter had ended no worse—and as they proceeded to gather up the "duds," they entered upon a discourse, wherein the rules of chivalry were gravely considered, and a decision soberly made, that there was no loss of honor in the affair; since such cases were of rare occurrence and did not happen under those circumstances by which a man's courage and valor were ordinarily tested.

On examining the lake, it was found that it was nearly surrounded by rocks, for the most part of perpendicular ascent, rising like a wall of masonry with its face to the lake, and from two to three hundred feet above the surface of the water. It was of oval form, and gave the appearance of an immense reservoir prepared by art—a section of its western wall, however, overhung the water, forming a high arched cavern beneath. No streams were discovered falling *into* the lake, but an outlet, running constantly *from* it, was noticed at the extreme south end, where the heights became depressed and fell to a level with the surface of this secluded yet interesting object of nature. A day spent in visiting this little lake will well repay the toil and labor it will cost.

Our travelers took an easterly direction from this point; and after undergoing the fatigue of the day, wearied to excess, hungry, chafed, and with their faces swollen from the bite of the poisonous flies, they arrived at night at an old hunter's lodge (near the lower falls of South Inlet) covered with bark, and as usual in such half-decayed shanties, filled with filth and vermin. Here necessity drove them to take up their quarters for the night—they accordingly struck up a fire, disposed of a few hard crackers, and a remnant of unsavory venison well jammed and mellowed, and before the light of day had fully disappeared, flung themselves down to rest. But the process of hardening against the bite of the flea, as a necessary preparation for sleep, was to be undergone; and while this was in progress, the agonizing knight of the pistol rolled over upon his back, drew up his knees, and with his journal and pencil in hand, gave vent to his experience in a poetical stanza—which he then and there entered down upon his diary, as follows:

"'In this rude spot, where weary pilgrims rest,
With bugs, and fleas, and fetid venison blessed,
With swollen limbs, unfit to rest or range,
We breathe the smoke of *Catamount Exchange.*
Meanwhile, our eyes are closed, by poisonous gnats and flies,
And' * * * * *

"It is proper to remark, that the interesting section of country connected with the Raquette is now flung open to easy access, by the recent completion of the Champlain and Carthage road, which passes near the northern shore of Raquette Lake. Light carriages, and teams with heavy loads, may pass from Lake Champlain, or the Black River valley, to this lake. Township forty, embracing the most desirable section of land in that vicinity, already contains a few families who have broken into the wilderness and commenced their improvements; and the prospect is, that this township will soon be occupied by prosperous and enterprising settlers Those who reside there, not only enjoy their beautiful localities, pure water, and healthful atmosphere, but their crops of Indian corn, wheat, potatoes, and garden vegetables. The first persons who came into this township were Messrs. Beach and Woods, who planted their rude dwelling upon Indian Point, commanding a most interesting view of the lake and its islands. The case of Mr. Woods should not pass unnoticed; as it furnishes an instance of man's capacity to overcome the serious deprivations rarely to be found. By exposure in the woods and snow through a cold winter's night, his feet and limbs were so badly frozen, that it became necessary to amputate both below the knee joints. Since that time he has used his knees as a substitute for feet; and, strange as it may seem, he follows his line of traps for miles through the wilderness, or with rifle in hand, hops through the woods in pursuit of deer. He may be seen plying his oars, and driving his little bark over the lakes and along the streams; and when he comes to a portage, the upturned boat will surmount his head, and take its course to the adjacent waters. His is a case that proves that there are instances in reality, 'where truth is stranger than fiction.'"

Yours, &c.

XXV.

SIGHTS AND SOUNDS—BEACH AND WOODS—A VISIT OF THIRTY MILES MADE BY A WOMAN.

Raquette Lake, August.

Dear H——:

You can spend days and weeks around the Raquette, sailing over its beautiful waters, penetrating its deep and quiet bays, taking trout at every cast of your line, aud killing a deer whenever you choose to put forth the effort. The sun rises on you from this green wilderness fresh as when it first looked on creation, and sets as lovingly in the mass of green, on the western slope, as though it had seen no sin and suffering in its course.

Let the light canoe rock awhile on the tiny waves that this glorious western breeze, redolent with the kiss of leaves, and pure from its long dalliance with nature, has set in motion. The shadows are flitting like sweet visions along that far-stretching slope of brilliant green, and disappear one after another over the summit. Yonder is a deer walking up and down the shore in the water, ever and anon lifting his antlered head, lest the garish day might reveal him to some lurking foe; and lo, there comes his consort, her white breast shining amid the leaves, as she also steps forth to drink. And here, out of this narrow cove, completely enveloped in bushes that sweep the water, and reeds that grow almost across its entrance —which seems to lurk in perpetual ambush on the shore—a wild duck from the Atlantic is leading forth her brood which she has hatched in this far-sequestered spot. What a chattering they make as they swim after the proud matron who is pushing boldly for a point near by. They move in the form of the figure V inverted, and the still water of the cove assumes the same shape clear to the shore. But the ever-watchful mother has caught sight of our boat, and prattling to her offspring, is off with incredible speed. She knows her young cannot fly, and hence will not rise herself from the water. True to her maternal instinct, she is willing to bide the worst, but both wings and fee: of the whole chattering squadron are in full play, making the lake foam where they pass. There, you are once more in the reeds, settling yourselves with a vast deal of self-congratulation into composure again, while your black heads and eyes turn and nod to catch the first approach of danger. Poor things, you are safe here; but next fall every rod of your flight from Montauk Point to Barnegat Bay, will be disturbed by the shot of the sportsman, and scarcely a pair of you will be left to revisit this far retreat again!

Vain dreaming this, I know, but the listless mood is upon me, and I cannot pull a strong and steady and *practical* stroke. The waves are out on a frolic—the deer stand idly lashing their tails in the water—the great, green forest just rustles to show that the leaves are all at play—the clouds move lazily across the sky and all nature seems dreaming in this fresh noon-day—and why should *I* not drink in the influence of the scene? I know a hard afternoon's toil is before me, and a bivouack on the ground at night, yet I seem enchained here by beauty. Sad thoughts and gentle feelings rise one after another an indistinguishable throng, and strange memories long since buried, come back with overpowering freshness. Here the great world of strife and toil speaks not, and its fierce struggles for gàin seem the madness of the maniac. You do not hate it—you pity it, and pity yourself that you ever loved it. The good you had forgotten returns, for nature wakes up the dead divinity within you, and rouses the soul to purer, nobler purposes. Besides, all things are free about me—the leap of the wave—the dash of the mountain stream—the flight of the eagle—the song of the wind, and the swaying of trees—all, all are free. Unmarred, unstained, the bright and happy world is spread out in my sight:

"Ah, when the wild turmoil of this wearisome life,
With its scenes of oppression, corruption, and strife;
The proud man's power, and the base man's fear—
The scorner's laugh, and the sufferer's tear—
And malice, and meanness, and falsehood, and folly,
Dispose me to musing and dark melancholy:
When my bosom is full, and my thoughts are high,
And my soul is sick with the bondman's sigh—
Oh, then, there is freedom, and joy, and pride,
Afar through the 'forest' alone to ride,
With the death-fraught firelock in my hand,
The only law of the desert land."

But to return to practical matters: yonder comes

the boat of Woods and Beach, the two solitary dwellers of this region. It is rather a singular coincidence that the only two inhabitants of this wilderness should be named *Woods* and *Beach.* I should not wonder if the next comers should be called "*Hemlock*" and "*Pine.*" These two men have killed hundreds of deer since they settled down here together, and a great many moose. Their leisure hours they spend in preparing the furs they have taken, and in tanning the deer skins, of which they make mittens. They need something during the long winter days and evenings for employment. When the snow is five feet deep on the level, and the ice three and four feet thick on the lake, and not the sign of a human footstep any where to be seen, the smoke of their cabin rises in the frosty air like a column in the desert—enhancing instead of relieving the solitude. The pitch pine supplies the place of candles, and the deep, red light from their humble window, at night, must present a singular contrast with the rude waste of snow, and the leafless forest around them.

When a quantity of these mittens are made up, Beach straps on his snow shoes, and with his trusty rifle in his hand, carries them out to the settlements, where they meet with a ready sale—for mittens made here in the woods are known to be "made upon honor." No buff-colored sheepskin comes from the shores of Raquette Lake, nor is the stout buckskin spoiled by destructive materials used to expedite the tanning.

Since the above was written, I am informed by my friend B—n that another family, composed of a man, his wife, and seven children, has emigrated to Raquette Lake. This woman—the only one now on the shores of the Raquette—took, last summer, an infant six months old, and a daughter fourteen years of age, and started for a clearing thirty miles distant, *on a visit.* Now carrying the boat on her head around the rapids—in one place two miles on a stretch while the girl lugged along the infant and oars—now stemming the swift current, and anon floating over the bosom of a calm lake, she pursued her toilsome way—accomplishing the *thirty miles by night.* What think you of that? As Captain Cuttle would say, "she is a woman as *is* a woman." To make a visit of thirty miles through an unbroken forest, with a babe six months old, and a girl only fourteen years of age, and carry and row her own boat the whole distance, is "spinning street yarn" on a large scale. I hope she had a glorious gossip to pay her for her trouble. It shows most conclusively that the visiting propensity, so strong in woman, is not a conventional thing, but inherent—belonging to her very nature.

This woman *deserves* to be the *first* on Raquette Lake. She bids fair to have seven children more, and I trust, when she dies, a monument will be erected to her memory.

Yours, &c.

XXVI.

MOOSE LAKES—"MURDERER'S POINT"—A GRAVE IN THE FOREST—TROUTING—A FAMILY OF THIRTEEN GIRLS—RIDING "BARE BACK"—A CURIOUS HORSE RACE.

August.

DEAR H——

FROM the Raquette your *nearest* way out of the woods is towards the Black River country. Ascending the Brown Tract Inlet four miles, you carry your boat over a portage two miles in extent to the Eighth Moose Lake, which forms the summit level of the waters of this region—those on the west flowing west into the Black River. This sheet of water is the first of a chain of lakes, eight in number, connected by streams, and forming a group of surpassing beauty. Being on the height of land, it is filled wholly by springs and rills, and of course its water is unrivalled in clearness and coldness. It is completely embosomed in trees, while a beach of sand, white as the driven snow, and almost as fine as table salt, shows between the green frame work of the forest and the lake, presenting a beautiful and strange contrast here in this land of rocks and cliffs. The bottom is composed of this white sand also, and can be seen through the clear water at an astonishing depth. In such cold water, with such a clear bottom, how can the trout be otherwise than delicious?

This charming sheet of water is about three miles in length, with an average width of a mile and a half.

The seven lakes that follow are not a mere repetition of the first, but vary both in size and shape, with a different frame-work of hills. The change is ever from beauty to beauty, yet a separate description would seem monotonous.

There they repose, like a bright chain in the forest, the links connected by silver bars. You row slowly through one to its outlet, and then, entering a clear stream, overhung with bushes, or fringed with lofty trees, seem to be suddenly absorbed by the wilderness. At length, however, you emerge as from a cavern, and lo! an untroubled lake, with all its variations of coast, and timber, and islands, greets the eye. Through this you also pass like one in a dream, wondering why such beauty is wasted where the eye of man rarely beholds it. Another narrow outlet receives you, and guiding your frail canoe along the rapid current, you are again swallowed up by the wilderness, to be born anew in a lovelier scene. Thus on, as if under a wizard's spell, you move along, alternately lost in the narrow channels, and struggling to escape the rocks on which the current would drive you, then floating over a broad expanse, extending as far as the eye can see into the mountains beyond.

A ride through these eight lakes is an episode in a man's life he can never forget. It furnishes a new experience—gives rise to a new train of thoughts and feelings, and opens to the dweller of our cities an entirely new world.

They vary in size from two to six miles, except the fifth and eighth, which are mere ponds. Thus, for more than twenty miles, you float through this primeval wilderness in a skiff that can be carried on the head, and yet are not compelled to take it from the water but once, the whole distance, and then only to pass over some five hundred yards.

Near the foot of the first lake, (or last in the route,) is "murderer's point," where a white man, some ten years since, shot an Indian. The latter, who was trapping around these waters, in some way gave offence to the white hunter, whose name was Johnson. A quarrel ensued, and the Indian was killed. Whether the murder was committed in the heat of a sudden fight, or in cold blood, is not known —the forest alone witnessed the bloody transaction: yet there, on the shore of that lonely river, sleeps the poor savage. A simple wooden cross, erected by some of his tribe, stands over the grave, awakening sad emotions in the breast of the wanderer. If it were on an open bank it would not seem so solitary, but surrounded as it is by an interminable forest, it looks fearfully forlorn.

By one of those singular discoveries which so often detect the murderer, Johnson was convicted of the crime. The people of Herkimer County, however, claiming him as their criminal, he was tried there and acquitted, and carried about the town on men's shoulders. The good Dutchmen of that county had suffered so much in former times from the depredations of the Indians, that they considered the man a public benefactor, rather than murderer, who slew one. To hang a man for killing an *Indian* was a monstrous absurdity—they would as soon think of punishing him for shooting a rattlesnake or wolf.

You cannot conceive the shock one feels in coming on a spot in the forest, where a murder has been committed. In the streets of a crowded city, or on the highway, all remembrance of the deed is soon effaced—changes take place, and the mere fact that ten thousand other things have transpired since it occurred, serves to weaken the associations connected with it, and indeed removes it much farther off. But in the still woods, the solitary grave and you are alone together. The motionless trunks seem stern watchers there; and you impart a consciousness to the sleeper, and imagine that the uneven surface around him was made by the fierce death-struggle, and that the leaves are yet tinted with his blood. I have often thought that a murderer in the heart of a boundless forest must feel more restless and wretched than if he were in a crowd of men. The suspicious eyes of his fellows could be encountered with far more firmness than those of that invisible presence which seems there to surround him. There is no way to escape himself —nothing to resist or to dare. "The scowl of revenge or stare of defiance, may be met, for there is a visible object" on which the passions can act; but to struggle with conscience—to hush the awful voice of *law* which God's universe about him is thundering in his ear, is a hopeless task.

Near the last of this chain of lakes is a small sheet of water called Moose Lake, from its being a favorite haunt of moose. Like the first mentioned in the group, it is embosomed in trees, but no mountains rise from its shores. It has also a beach of incomparable whiteness, and the bottom of the lake looks like a vast bed of fine white salt. As you sit in your boat, you can see it glittering beneath at an immense depth, while ever and anon a huge trout flits like a shadow over it. A certain judge and his lady are accustomed in summer to come from the western settlements, and camp out for two or three weeks at a time on its shores, and fish. The lady, accomplished and elegant, enjoys the recreation amazingly, and once caught herself a trout weighing *nineteen pounds*

There are no islands upon it, but a ong green promontory almost cuts it in two, from which you get an entrancing view of the whole lake.

My friend B——n, with a hunter, had great sport here one day. He did not fish over an hour, and yet in that short time, took a *hundred and twenty pounds* of trout, and left them biting as sharp and fast as when he began. Going back through the lake towards Brown's tract, two moose with their broad-spreading horns and huge black forms, were seen standing on the shore. They can see to an astonishing distance; and at the first glimpse of the boat, they wheeled into the woods and made off. One, however, was killed the next day. Deer were stumbled on almost every half mile. B——n said he counted six, two of which the rifle of the hunter fetched down. A deer seems unable to measure distance correctly on the water, or else reasons very poorly on what he sees; for if a man will approach noiselessly and without changing his posture, he can often, in broad daylight, get within fair shooting range.

To strike through the woods, it is only about five miles from the head of this lake to "Brown's tract," as it is called, where the signs of civilized life first appear, though it will be a great mistake if when you get here you imagine yourself "*out of the woods*"—a long road yet remains to be traveled.

This "tract" receives its name from John Brown, formerly governor of Rhode Island. Some fifty years ago, he bought two hundred thousand acres here—all wilderness—with the intention of forming a large settlement. By presents of land and putting up at his own expense, mills and a forge for the manufacture of iron, he induced many families to migrate—at one time, it is said, there were thirty located in this solitary spot. But at that period, there was not a single public improvement west of Albany, hence there were no facilities for getting to market. Added to this, the land was cold and unproductive—the winters long and severe, which so disheartened the settlers that they one after another left. Governor Brown, who had constantly furnished large supplies at length died, and then the colony broke up.

Three thousand acres had been cleared up, which now lies a vast common, with only one inhabitant to cultivate it. He occupies it without being owner, yet pays no rent, and no taxes: the Robinson Crusoe of this little territory, he has what he can raise, and no one to dispute his domain. The log dwellings of the settlers have all rotted away—the mills fallen in upon the mill stones, and the forge upon the hammers. One house alone, which formerly belonged to the agent, remains standing; and in this Arnold and his family reside. Boonville, twenty miles distant, is the nearest settlement. Yet here he lives contented, year after year, with his family of thirteen children—twelve girls and one boy—by turns trapping, shooting and cultivating his fields. The agricultural part, however, is performed mostly by the females who plow, sow, rake, bind, &c., equal to any farmer. Two of the girls threshed alone, with common flails, *five hundred* bushels of oats in one winter, while their father and brother were away trapping for marten. Occupying such a large tract of land, and cultivating as much as he chooses, he is able to keep a great many cattle, and has some excellent horses which these girls of his ride with a wildness and recklessness that makes one tremble for their safety. You will often see five or six of them, each on her own horse, some astraddle, and some sideways, yet all "bare back;" i. e. without any saddle, racing it like mad creatures over the huge common. They sit (I was going to say their saddles) their horses beautifully; and with their hair streaming in the wind, and dresses flying about their white limbs and bare feet, careering across the plains, they look wild and spirited enough for Amazons. They frequently ride without a bridle or even halter, guiding the horse by a motion or stroke of the hand. What think you of a dozen fearless girls mounted on fleet horses, without a saddle, on a dead run? I should like to see them going down Broadway. Yet they are modest and retiring in their manners, and mild and timid as fawns among strangers.

There was a lad about nineteen years of age with my friend B——n, whom one of these girls challenged to a race. He accepted it, and they whipped their horses to the top of their speed. The barn, nearly a mile distant, was to be the goal. Away they went, pell-mell—the girl without a saddle, across the field. The boy plied the whip lustily, ashamed to be beaten by a woman, yet he fell behind, full a hundred yards. Mortified at his discomfiture, and the peal of laughter that went up, he hung his head, saying it was no fault of his, for she had the best horse. She then offered to exchange with him, and try the race over. This was fair, and he was compelled to accept the second challenge. Taking their old station, they started again. It would have done a jockey good to have seen that stout frontier youth use his whip, and beat his horse's ribs with his heels, and heard him yell. But all would not do—that girl sat quietly leaning over her steed's neck ; and with her low, clear chirrup, and her sharp, well-planted blows inspired the beaten animal with such courage and speed, that he seemed to fly over the ground, and she came out full as far ahead as before. The poor fellow had to give up beaten, humiliating as it was, and the girl with a smile of triumph, slipped the bridle from her nag's head, and turned him loose in the fields to graze.

The mother, however, is the queen of all woodman's wives—but you must see her and hear her *talk*, to appreciate her character. If she will not stump the coolest, most hackneyed man of the world that ever faced a woman, I will acknowledge myself to have committed a very grave error of judgment.

Her husband's "*saple line*," as she termed it, (sable line,) that is line of trapping, is thirty miles long, and he is often absent on it several days at a time.

It is thirty miles through the woods to Boonville,

from whence you can easily make your way to Rome.

My next will be on my return route through Forked and Long Lakes, and the woods to Warren County.

Yours truly.

XXVII.

LOST IN THE WOODS—AN OLD INDIAN AND HIS DAUGHTER—FAREWELL TO MITCHELL—MOSQUITOES AND BLACK FLIES.

In the Woods, August.

Dear H——:

It was with weary forms and saddened hearts that we left this morning our encampment on Forked Lake, and turned the prows of our boats homeward. A person who has never traveled in the woods, cannot appreciate the feelings of regret with which one leaves the spot where he has once pitched his tent. The half-extinguished firebrands scattered around—the broken sticks that for the time being seemed valuable as silver forks, and the deserted shanty, all have a desolate appearance, and it seems like forsaking trusty friends, to leave them there alone in the forest.

The morning was sombre, and the wind fresh as we

pulled down the lake, and again entered the narrow river that pierced so adventurously the dark bosom of the forest. The fatiguing task of carrying our boats was performed over again, with the additional burden of a deer we had partially consumed. At one portage P——, with two rifles and an overcoat as his part of the freight, started off in advance of the rest. We were each of us too much engaged with our own affairs to notice the direction he took ; but supposing, of course, he was ahead, pushed on. But as we came to the next launching place, he was nowhere to be found. "He has gone on, I guess," said one, "to the next carrying place." We shouted, but the echo of our own voices was the only reply the sullen woods sent back, and one was despatched farther on to ascertain whether our conjecture was true. The report was soon brought back that P—— was nowhere to be found. I, by this time, began to feel somewhat alarmed, for the *lost one was my brother*, and taking Mitchell with me, hastened back towards the spot where he had parted from us. I shouted aloud, but the deep waterfall drowned my voice, and its monotonous roar seemed mocking my anxious halloo. I then fired my rifle, but the sharp report was followed only by its own echo. Mitchell then discharged his, and after listening anxiously awhile, we heard a shot far up the river. Soon after, "bang, bang," went two more guns in the same direction The poor fellow had heard our shots, and fearing we might not hear *his* in return, and hence take a wrong direction in pursuit of him, just stood, and loaded and fired as fast as he could. When we found him he was as pale as marble, and looked like one who had been in a state of complete bewilderment. On leaving us, instead of going down stream as he should have done, he turned directly up. After awhile he came out on the bank of, to him, a strange river. As it was on the wrong side to be the one we had floated down, he thought he must have crossed over to another, but finally concluded it would be the safest course to retrace his steps. This he was doing to the best of his ability when he heard our rifle shots. We scolded him for his stupidity in thus causing us alarm and delay, which, he very coolly remarked was neither very just nor sensible, and then trudged on.

One gets lost in the woods when he least expects it. Awhile ago, a man from the settlements, a hunter, too, left the shores of Long Lake, with a dog to start a deer on the mountain, for a friend who was to watch in the boat. He left his rifle behind him so as to climb the mountain more easily, but after beating about awhile, got lost. Three days after the hound came home with a long gash in his side, and in a week or so more the body of the master was found on the shore of the lake. The dog evidently clung to him faithfully, till the man—having no gun with which to kill game—had endeavored to stab him for food. With this he left him, and the poor wretch wandered about, till prostrated by hunger, he laid down and died.

Towards night B——n and myself arrived with Mitchell at his hut, where he found his aged Indian father and young sister waiting his return. "Old Peter," as he is called, is now over eighty years of age. He shakes with the palsy, and is constantly muttering to himself in a language half French and half Indian, while his daughter scarcely twenty years old, is silent as a statue. She is quite pretty, and her long hair is not straight like that of her race, but hangs in waving masses around her bronzed neck and shoulders. She will speak to no one, not even to answer a question, except to her father and brother.

I have tried in vain to make her say no or yes, but she invariably turns to her father or Mitchell, and makes them answer. This old man still roams the forest, and stays where night overtakes him.

It was sad to look upon his once powerful frame, now bowed and tottering, while his thick gray hair hung like a huge mat around his wrinkled and seamed visage. His tremulous hand and faded eye could no longer send the unerring rifle ball to its mark, and he was compelled to rely on a rusty fowling-piece. Everything about him was in keeping—even his dog was a mixture of the wolf and dog, and was the quickest creature I ever saw move: his very gambols frightened me, for when leaping to a caress, his bound was so quick and eager, that he seemed about to tear me in pieces—indeed it was always a dubious matter with me, when I approached him, whether he intended to play or fight.

But poor old Peter cannot stand another winter, I fear,—and some lonely night, in the lonely forest, that dark-haired maiden will see him die, far from human habitations; and her slender arm will carry his corpse many a weary mile, to rest among his tribe. As I have seen her decked out with water-lilies paddling that old man over the lake, I have sighed over her fate. She seems wrapt up in him, and to have but one thought—one purpose of life—to guard and nurse her parent. The hour that sees her sitting by the camp-fire beside her dead father, will witness a grief as intense and desolate as ever visited a more cultivated bosom. God help her then. I can conceive of no sadder sight than that forsaken maiden, in some tempestous night, sitting all in the forest, holding the dead or dying head of her father, while the moaning winds sing his dirge, and the flickering fire sheds a ghastly light on the scene.

How strong is habit. That old man cannot be persuaded to sit down in peace beneath a quiet roof—ministered to and cherished as his wants require—but still clings to his wandering life, and endures hunger, cold, and fatigue, and wanders houseless and homeless. He continues to hunt, though his shot seldom strikes down a deer; and he still treads the forest, though his trembling limbs but half perform their office, and his aged shoulders groan under the burden of his light canoe. I saw him looking at a handful of specimens of birch bark he had collected, and balancing which to choose as material for a new canoe. He still looks forward to years of hunting, and days of toil, when the bark of life is already touching those dark waters that roll away from this world and all it contains.

Aug. 31.—Yesterday as I was leaving Long Lake, I met the old Indian and his daughter just starting on their return journey of a hundred and fifty miles. The father was sitting in the middle of the bark canoe on the bottom, while the daughter occupied the stern and paddled the boat. Her head was uncovered, and her long hair which almost swept the water, was filled with white lilies she had plucked by the shore. Noiseless and steady swept on the frail craft, impelled by her sinewy arm—stretching down the middle of the lake towards the dark outlet. It was a sad sight to behold spring and winter thus united, one decked out in flowers and the other covered with the frosts of time, and know the fate before them. I watched their lessening forms till they were a mere speck in the distance, and then struck across the lake and began my fifty miles stretch through the woods.

Mitchell accompanied us several miles on our way,

as if loth to leave us. In parting I gave him a canister of powder, a pocket compass, and a small spy-glass, to keep as mementos of me, and shook his honest hand with as much regret as I ever did that of a white man. I shall long remember him—he is a man of deeds and not of words—kind, gentle, delicate in his feelings, honest and true as steel. I would start on a journey of a thousand miles in the woods with him alone, without the slightest anxiety, although I carried a million of dollars about my person. I never lay down beside a trustier heart than his, and never slept sounder than I have with one arm thrown across his brawny chest.

There is one thing I have not mentioned, which mars very much a tramp through these woods—I mean the mosquitoes and black flies. The latter disappear about the first of July, but the former are like the locusts of Egypt. However, I was troubled less than I anticipated—on the lakes the fresh wind drives them away, and at night your camp fire keeps them off. In the woods of a damp, still morning, or just at evening, away from a fire, they assail one by battalions. Hence, fishing along the inlets or outlets is often a protracted agony. I once stood on a rock and dragged my fly over a pool so crowded with trout that half a dozen would be on the surface at once, and yet by the time I had taken ten or fifteen, I was compelled to fling down my rod and run and scream, for the blood was pouring in rivulets from my neck, face and hands. If, however, you are where you can sit in a boat, by placing some earth in the bottom of it, and building a little fire, (a "smudge,") you may fish quite comfortably.

I mention the mosquitoes solely to relieve my conscience, so that no one—if any may be tempted here by my descriptions—shall say I have deceived him. However, I never suffered more from their bite than I have on Long Island. A green veil wrapped around the face and neck when traveling, is often a great protection.

Sept. 1. The fifty miles of forest were safely made, and with a pair of antlers on one side of my saddle, and a noble pheasant I shot with my rifle, on the other, I landed at an humble dwelling where I had left my traps, and was soon accoutered again like a civilized man.

Yours truly.

Durand. Burt.

LAKE SCHROON.

XXVIII.

SCHROON LAKE—A NUT FOR SPORTSMEN—WOODS ON FIRE.

SCHROON LAKE.

DEAR H——:

LAKE SCHROON is some nine miles long, gently waving in its shape and dotted with green islands. Some have compared it to Lake Como—from one point it bears an exact resemblance in shape to the neck of a swan. It is a most beautiful sheet of water—the shores sloping down to it on one side like those of Skaneateles, and a bold mountain kneeling in it on the other. At the foot is the residence of Mr. Benthuysen, commanding one of the finest views I have ever seen. The lake here is narrow, and as it half encircles the house, it looks like the Hudson River in its windings. There could hardly be a more picturesque situation for a summer residence; and in England it would soon be crowned by a magnificent pile of buildings. The lake should be called "Scaroon," from a French family that first gave it the name—the rapid way of pronouncing it has changed it into Schroon. The water is very pure and cold, and salmon trout were once found in it in abundance. Latterly, however, they have become more scarce, so four years since some men living on its banks got a few pickerel and put them in as a basis of a new stock of fish. It was agreed on all hands not to take any out for four years. The time being expired this spring, they commenced spearing them, and the quantities they have caught almost surpasses belief. Hundreds of pounds have been taken, some of the fish, weighing *twelve and thirteen pounds.* The rapidity with which they bred is equalled only by the ratio of increase in size, for a growth of four pounds per annum in weight is almost incredible. It was doubtless owing to the abundance and richness of the food and the perfect adaptness of the water to their wants and habits. Fish of all kinds are easily affected by the place they are in, and the quantity and kind of food with which they are supplied. A trout kept in a well, though fed ever so bounteously will scarcely gain a pound in three years, while I have seen those that weighed two ounces in June, by having fine food and water, weigh six in August. The spawn that run up the cool streamlets into meadows where the water is always fresh and filled with worms or grasshoppers, will *treble their size* in two months. There is another curious fact about trout and pickerel as well as some other species of fresh water fish—their size will vary in proportion to the magnitude of the pond or lake they inhabit. Thus you will find in two lakes in Massachusetts, lying side by side—one, a half a mile round, and the other three miles, the same fish differing altogether in size. In the latter you will take a great many pickerel weighing three and four pounds, and now and then one much larger, while in the former the average weight will be from eight to eighteen ounces.

THE WOODS ON FIRE.

Last night witnessed a scene of sublimity that baffles all attempts to describe it worthily—for the forests all around were a mass of surging, tossing, billowy flame. I have seen the woods on fire upon Long Island, when the flames traveled so rapidly that a man on horseback could scarcely, at an easy gallop, keep ahead of them—and it was a grand spectacle. The vast columns of smoke rolling into the heavens, yet leaning eagerly forward, as if straining on the chase—the lambent tongues of flame, shooting at intervals above the murky mass that hugged the tree tops, and the steady roar, like that of the surge, filled me with new ideas of terror and sublimity. The rabbits and foxes in countless numbers, smelling the danger from afar, scoured the thickets in every direction—the deer ran frightened from their haunts, and nature herself seemed to stand aghast at the fury of the devouring element. But the leaves and shrubs alone fed the flames—the tall trees were only scathed and blackened, which, together with the lowness of the land, lessened and concealed the effect of the scene.

A prairie on fire is simply a mass of flame, rushing like a race horse over the ground—terrible to behold, but exhibiting a sameness in its aspect that leaves no room to the imagination. But a mountain of magnificent timber ablaze is another matter—from base to ridge your eye takes in the whole extent, and you look on a bosom of fire, from which rise waving columns and lofty turrets of flame.

There has been a long drought in this section, which so dried up everything combustible, that the forest became one great tinder box, needing only a spark to make a conflagration. This was accidentally furnished by some men burning a fallow. First a column of blue smoke began to ascend through the trees, which rapidly swelled in size and increased in velocity, until at length the fire got under way, and took up its fierce march, and by night the whole mountain was wrapt in a fiery mantle. It came roaring down to the clearing where I stood, threatening to leap over the narrow barrier, in its eagerness to burst all bonds that would restrain it. Trees a hundred feet high, and five and six and eight feet in circumference, were on fire from the root to the top—vast pyramids of flame, now surging in the eddies of air that caught them, now bending as if about to yield the struggle, then lifting superior to the foe, and dying, martyr-like, in the vast furnace. One tree enlisted for awhile all my sympathies—it was a noble stem, and stood for a long time erect and motionless amid the enveloping smoke and flame, sometimes buried from my sight and then appearing again—its black form looming mysteriously through the murky cloud that shrouded it, as though defying its enemy. Even after the blaze had curled itself around the entire trunk, and run out to the extreme limits of the branches, it still retained its calm and dignified aspect —its head, and body, and arms reaching out into the night, all on fire, and yet scorning to show signs of pain. At length, however, the heat seemed to have reached its vitals, for it suddenly swung backward, as if in agony, while a shower of embers fell like sky rockets around the blazing outline, to its roots. Shorn of its glory, the flashing, trembling form stood thus awhile, crisping and writhing in the blaze, till weary with its long suffering, it threw itself with a sudden and hurried sweep, on the funeral pile around. From the noble pine to the bending sprout, the trees were aflame, while the crackling underbrush seemed a fiery net-work cast over the prostrate forms of the monarchs of the forest. When the fire caught a dry stub, it ran up the huge trunk like a serpent, and, coiling around the withered branches, shot out its fiery tongue as if in mad joy, over the raging element below; while ever and anon, came a crash that reverberated far away in the gorges—the crash of falling trees, at the overthrow of which there went up a cloud of sparks and cinders and ashes. Sweeping along on its terrible path, the tramp of that conflagration filled the air with an uproar like the bursting of billows on a rocky shore.

In one direction the forest made down into a valley through which coursed a rapid stream, on the farther side of which arose a mountain of rocks, almost naked from base to summit. Trees and shrubs, however, had grown in the interstices, but the drought had killed them all, and the white and withered stems could scarcely be distinguished from the bleached rocks against which they grew.

Along this valley the conflagration swept; and, skirting the bank of the stream with fearful velocity, and licking up everything to the water's brink; went for a while careering onward as if satisfied with the field before it. But suddenly there seemed to be a division of the forces—while one portion was content with a direct invasion, the other made a halt as if resolved on a more desperate attack. The white, dry mountain on the opposite side of the stream had attracted its attention; and clearing the channel with one bold bound, it began to scale the opposing cliffs. As the flames got amongst this vast collection of combustible matter, they raged with a strength and fury to which all their former madness seemed placidity. Have you ever in a still summer day heard the roar of a coming hurricane? if so, you have a faint conception of the terrific rushing sound of the fire as it wrapped those mountains. It was near midnight, and that rocky ridge became in the gloom a vast elevation of fire—laced with lines of fire of brighter hue, and shooting up jets of flame against the murky sky, as if resolved to assail the heavens also. As I stood gazing on this wild spectacle, and listening to its wilder uproar, suddenly a shrill and distant scream cleaved the flames, and was borne with startling clearness through the air. Some wild animal, probably a panther, had been roused from his sleep by the heat, but awoke only to find himself hemmed in on every side by a burning wall. Bounding madly from side to side, he had at last sprang into the fire, and that last cry was his death shriek.

This morning, a black and smouldering mass alone remains of last night's wild work. Trees half burnt in two, others broken off at the middle, and all smoking amidst the devastation, present a most forlorn aspect in the bright morning air.

The backwoodsman never sees a city on fire, but he beholds a far more imposing spectacle. Around the haunts of men the devouring element is everywhere met by resistance. Not only do solid walls obstruct its progress, but human effort fights it at every step, subduing its fury and lessening its force. But in the woods it has free scope—no arm arrests it—no confinement smothers its rage. Free as the forest it ranges, it puts forth all its energy, and is fanned into greater fury, by the wind, itself creates.

Thus, my friend, do scenes of beauty and terror succeed each other on the margin and in the heart of the wilderness. There is no monotony in nature and no lack of excitement.

Yours truly.

XXIX.

LUMBERMEN—A STUDENT AND HUNTER OUTWITTED BY A PROFESSOR—A PHILOSOPHICAL HUSBAND—A PROSPECTIVE WIDOW LOOKING OUT FOR HER OWN INTEREST.

Schroon Lake, August.

Dear H——:

After the description I have given of the wilderness and its extent, I seem to hear you inquiring, "What do people live on there?" Well, not much of anything; yet money is made in this region—that is, out nearer the settlements. You have no conception of the quantity of lumber that is taken every winter from some part of this vast plateau to Albany. A thousand people will be in these woods, where, in the summer, there is not a living being. Speculators buy the land for the sake of the timber, and then in the winter carry in provisions, etc., for the lumbermen who are to cut it. Log huts are put up in the sheltered gorges for themselves and cattle, and some poles driven into the logs for bedsteads; and thus equipped and encamped, they lay siege to the pines. Teams are made to work, and logs are drawn, where you would say it was impossible for cattle to stand. A great deal of land is bought of government solely for the pine on it; and after that is cut down, it is allowed to revert back to the State to pay its taxes. In the more central regions, however, there is no timber cut, as it is impossible to get it out to market: but as civilization extends, the interior of the Empire State will, no doubt, be reached by roads, or water navigation.

Speaking of living, reminds me of an anecdote related to me by a professor of mathematics in one of our colleges. Sent here for scientific purposes, he took with him as a companion a younger brother who had just graduated, and an old hunter, for a guide, cook, and provider-general. Passing one day a clearing, in which some fine peas were growing, they purchased a small quantity to give relish to a dinner some time in the forest. Not long after, being fatigued by a hard forenoon's work, they pitched their camp on the borders of a lonely lake, and the professor said,

"Come, let us have those peas to-day." So while he was taking some observations down by the lake, the old hunter and the young graduate prepared the dinner. After a while (the professor told me) he noticed an unusual chuckling between the student and the backwoodsman. Suspecting some trickery, he strolled quietly up towards the fire, as if endeavoring to get a new point of observation, but in fact to watch narrowly their proceedings. Supposing that the professor was deep in equations and angles and mathematical lines, they relaxed their caution, and he observed that they were making wooden spoons with their penknives. All at once it flashed on him that he and they had nothing but penknives to eat the peas with, and that here was a conspiracy to rob him of his share. Saying nothing, he walked back to the lake shore, and picking up one of those large muscle shells which are found in all our fresh water lakes and rivers, and will hold more than an ordinary spoon, he fitted a split stick to it for a handle, and clapped them both in his pocket. Then sauntering back in order to prevent them making very extensive preparations, he kept around, until the dinner was cooked His presence restricted very much their operations, and they were able to finish but very shallow spoons after all. The peas being at length done, they were poured into the common dish, and lo! it was all *soup*. To prevent the possibility of the professor's getting even a moiety, they had cooked them so that the peas were like Virgil's "*rari nantes in gurgite vasto.*"

Imagine them now all seated on the ground around their food, each stabbing with his penknife at the peas, which dodge under the surface at every blow, like frogs when pelted with stones by mischievous boys. After this ridiculous process had been carried on awhile, to the ill-suppressed merriment of the student and hunter, they whipped out their wooden spoons, and flourishing them over their heads with a loud "hurrah," made a dive at the peas. The professor said nothing, but coolly drawing forth his huge muscle shell and stick, and fitting them together, began to ladle up the soup. The hunter and graduate stopped in utter amazement at this new development, and with their spoons suspended half way to their mouths, gazed with blank countenances at the quiet professor, who, without uttering a word, or changing a feature, diligently plied his shell. By his accurate and mathematical mode of ladling, he was enabled to take up an enormous quantity at every dip, and in a few moments every pea had vanished. The whole operation had been carried on with the sobriety with which he would have reduced an equation, while the hunter and student looked inquiringly at each other, yet without venturing a word of expostulation against the strange proceeding. When the last pea disappeared, he looked up as much as to say, "Is there anything more to eat, gentlemen?" This was carrying out the joke so capitally that the two conspirators were compelled to laugh. The old hunter, as he licked his empty spoon, confessed that for once he had been outwitted.

The other day I took a heavy boot to a shoemaker, or rather *mender*, to be repaired before I set forth on a new expedition, of whom I was told a capital anecdote. An English emigrant had settled down in a remote part of the forest, where he cleared a little space about him and built a log hut. He had been there but a year or two, when one day as he was absent in the woods with his eldest daughter, his hut took fire and burned down. His wife was sick, but she managed to crawl out, taking the straw bed on which she lay with her. At evening the husband returned to find his house in ruins. It was a winter night, and the snow lay deep on the ground. Calling aloud, he heard a faint voice reply, and going in the direction from which it came, found his wife stretched on the bed in the snow. Getting together a few boards left from the conflagration, he made a shelter over her. That night she was safely delivered of a child which survived and is now living. But under the exposure and excitement together, the husband took a violent cold, which, having fastened on his lungs, and being resisted by no medical treatment whatever, terminated in the consumption. He, however, reared another hut, and during the summer a young settler came in and purchased a tract near by him. His being the only family within a long distance, this backswoodsman often passed the evening in their society. It was not long before he discovered that his neighbor could not long survive, for the most ignorant in this region know all the symptoms of pulmonary disease which carries off three-fourths of those who die. Accompanying this conclusion came naturally the reflection, what would become of the wife; and as she was good-looking and industrious he thought he could not do better than marry her himself. Acting on this consideration, he mentioned the matter to her, remarking that her husband could not live long, and asking if she would marry him after he was dead?

She replied that she had no objections at all if "*her husband was willing.*" He said he had no doubt on that point, and he would speak to him about it. He did so, and the husband unhesitatingly gave his consent, adding that he was glad she would be so well provided for after his death. So when winter approached, the young settler would come and "court" the prospective widow, while the dying husband laid and coughed on the bed in the corner.

Now there was not much sentiment in this, I grant, but there was a vast deal of philosophy. It was rather cool on her part, to be sure, but vastly sensible on his. What could his wife and children do, all alone there in the woods, without a protector? The toughest part of the proceeding, and that which no doubt tested the backwoodsman's philosophy the severest, was the *courtship.* To lie gasping for breath in one part of the room, and see the young athletic and healthy backwoodsman and his wife sitting together by the fire, and know that after a few more painful weeks, he would occupy that place permanently, and yet bear it all patiently, required a good deal of stamina. Especially must the reflection that they were both probably very anxious to have him take his departure, have been rather a bitter pill to swallow. I go into all these little particulars, you know, to show the character of my hero to the best advantage—*the heroine speaks for herself.* These two interesting personages were my shoemaker and his wife.

Yours truly,

XXX.

ODDS AND ENDS—TRIAL OF A THIEF IN THE BACK-WOODS—NEW MODE OF REPORTING AN ELECTION—PARADOX LAKE—VON RAUMER AND HIS STATEMENTS.

DEAR H——:

THEY have a curious way of disposing of civil and political matters in the backwoods; for they are not trammelled by the *formalities* of law, having imbibed the very ridiculous notion that its *end* is secured by the administration of *justice*. It will be some time, I am afraid, before they become sufficiently educated to understand that the science of law as reduced to practice now-a-days, is based on two great principles—first, to give the scoundrel a better chance than the honest man—and second, to make technicalities weigh against truth and justice. The idea never entered their heads, poor souls, that a slight informality should *always* be sufficient to defeat the cause of a good man, and advance that of a bad one.

Being so barbarous as to love simple justice, some of their trials are conducted on a singular plan. On one occasion, a little settlement of some half a dozen families having discovered a thief among their number, without farther ado, assembled, tried, and condemned him. The nearest jail, however, was fifty miles distant, through the forest: yet they resolved to despatch him thither, and two men were appointed as his conductors.

The first day they made about twenty-five miles, and then built up a fire and lay down for the night, with their prisoner. In the morning, feeling rather stiff and lame, they declared that the tramp of a hundred miles was going to cost more than it would come to, and so turned him loose in the woods to find his way out as he best could.

I was much amused at a method of voting adopted in another settlement composed of a few clearings—the only ones in the township—in which were some ten or a dozen voters. The candidate for their suffrages—I forget his name—lived in Glen's Falls, near Saratoga Springs. Having assembled together in one of the log huts of the settlers, they talked over the matter, and finally concluded to vote all one way, and for this gentleman. It was a grave and solemn deliberation, and the sound political maxims there uttered were worthy of the momentouso ccasion that called them together. Having folded up their some dozen votes, they put them in a little wooden box with a lid to it, and despatched a man with them eighty miles distant to Glen's Falls, fifty of which were through a dense forest. After several days' hard traveling, he reached the place; but instead of going to the proper authorities, he went straight to the candidate's house, and opening the box, counted the votes saying, "Here, them's all for you—every one of 'em." The man laughed, and said that he was much obliged for the votes, but they could do him no good, brought in this informal way.

I caught a terrible drubbing in a school house, the other day, from a Methodist exhorter. Seeing me present, and hearing or surmising that I was from New York, he thought it was a good opportunity to give his opinion of the inhabitants of that wicked city. Among other severe things which he uttered, he said the people were so affected that they could not say "*Tuesday*," but must say '*Chuseday*," and could not say INK, "like a man, but *writin' fluid*." I fairly writhed under the scorching rebuke, feeling as I often have done under some of the criticisms on my books in the Magazines. I have no doubt *he* also felt very much as the writer or penny-a-liner did, who concocted those annihilating reviews. It reminded me of an article I once saw in the "New Englander," written by an ignorant conceited clergyman, who, irritated by the itching after notoriety, was willing to expose his folly, if he only could be talked about. I forget the article, but I remember one sentence, over which I had a hearty laugh—first, at the long ears, which everywhere stuck out, and second, at the ludicrous gravity with which I knew he contemplated the feat he had performed, while his readers were smiling at his stupidity. He was reviewing my "Napoleon and his Marshals," and among other defects, (some of which he made up deliberately,) he said I used the phrase "delivered battle," which was entirely wrong. He condemned it, intimating that it was very corrupt English, unscholarlike and *vicious*"—when he ought to have known it was a *technical military phrase*, for which I was no more responsible than for the phrase "*artillery practice*," or "*advancing en echelon*," and which is perfectly proper, as any, but an ignoramus knows. "Delivered battle!" "very bad English"—ah, he said "*writin' fluid*," he did not say "*ink!*" So another critic rebuked me for using the word "*stand-point*"—saying I should have written "*standing point!!!*" How very *small a dog can bark!*

A few miles from the head of Schroon Lake is Lake Paradox, which derives its name from the fact that its waters flow *two ways.* Its outlet empties into the east branch of the Hudson (i. e.) in ordinary times. But when, as it frequently happens in the spring, the river suddenly rises even with its banks, its surface is above the level of the lake, which, of course, swells much slower. The current of the outlet is then reversed and flows back into the lake. This double motion of the stream has given it the name "Paradox."

BURLINGTON.

I came across the country to Lake Champlain, taking some fine trout on the way. About six miles from Crown Point, I for the first time in my life caught a full view of the Green Mountains of Vermont. They were a long way off, but in the bright light of the setting sun, their bold outline showed beautifully against the clear sky. I was struck with the soft, blue coloring over them, like that we so often see in Italy, and which is generally thought to be peculiar to that country. Burlington is one of the most beautiful places on the continent, though I was provoked with a remark made by Prof. Von Raumer one day in company with some of the professors of the college. He said he had traveled from Boston through the Atlantic States to New Orleans, and up the Mississippi, through Canada, and back to Vermont; and that Niagara and Burlington furnished the only scenery that could be called fine he had found in all his route. Now so old a traveler as Von Raumer ought to be ashamed of such a remark. If he will go through the country on railroads and steamboats, at the rate of fifteen and twenty miles an hour, he should not complain of dearth of scenery. I have seen both continents, (not excepting even the Professor's favorite Germany,) and I affirm that in *natural scenery* the United States stands unrivalled; and if this remark is an index of the book he designs to publish about us, I would not give a straw for it. How supremely foolish for a man to hurry through the country by steam, taking all the lowland in his route, and then pretend to write about our scenery. These three months' tourists are not the most reliable in the world. To add to the Professor's wisdom, he took the *night* boat up the lake. Very likely he went *down* the *Hudson* by night also. Suppose he had gone up by daylight, and across the country from Burlington to Boston, and then through Massachusetts and Connecticut to Albany, and down the Hudson on a pleasant day—every hour would have been crowded with rich and varied scenery.

A man who should visit Switzerland and never go into the Oberland or Tyrol, and then say there was no scenery in the country that could be called sublime, would be deemed insane—but a foreign traveler no more thinks of visiting the wild and almost untrodden portions of our land, than he does of committing suicide. He expects to see everything worth seeing, without leaving the lines of railroads, or going beyond the precincts of good hotels. As well might a man give an opinion of the scenery of the Highlands after passing only from Edinburgh to Glasgow, as speak of that of our country after traveling only on the great thoroughfares that intersect it. Our gorges are yet dark with fir trees, amid which the seeker after natural beauty must sleep—our heaven piercing mountains encircled by vast forests or broader deserts through which he must toil, if he would reach the commanding summits.

Yours truly,

XXXI.

AUTUMN A PAINTER—MANNER OF WORKING.

> Leaves have their time to fall,
> And flowers to wither at the North wind's breath."

DEAR H——:

No country can compare with ours in the richness, at least of its *autumn* scenery. The mountains of the eastern world are not wooded like ours, and hence cannot exhibit such a mass of foliage as they present. But if you wish to behold autumn in its glory, you must stand on some height that overlooks this vast wilderness. What seemed to you in summer an interminable sea of green, becomes a limitless expanse of the richest colors—a vast collection of fragmentary rainbows. And the different effects of *light* on different portions is most astonishing. Here a mountain blazes in splendor, and there a valley looks like a kaleidescope—just so variegated and confused.

Autumn has been written and rhymed about from the days of Thomson down, but always in the same general tone of sadness. The text of every one has been—

> "The melancholy days have come—
> The saddest of the year."

There must be something natural in this, or it would not be so universal; and my own experience has heretofore corresponded with this prevailing sentiment. Indeed the effect of the dying year is palpable on those least affected by such changes and least conscious of them. You notice it in the very sports of children. In spring time the most vigorous games and boisterous merriment are seen on every village green. But in autumn these are thrown aside for forest strolls or walks by the river side. The scene subdues and chastens the very spirit of childhood; and there *is* something sad in seeing the glorious summer, that has been so full of life and health and beauty, lie down and die on the bosom of Nature. Hope, which comes with spring, yields in autumn to reflection, and man looks forward to decay rather than to maturity and strength. But this feeling becomes deeper and sadder as one enters the forest and hears the leaves rustling to his tread, and the sound of the squirrel cracking the nuts amid the dying tree-tops.

The trees have a melancholy aspect about them—they appear to be conscious that their glory is departing; and every leaf, as it loosens itself from the stem where it has nodded and swayed the livelong summer in joy, and flutters to the earth, seems to lie down as a sad memorial of the departing year.

But for once in autumn I have had none of these feelings. Roaming through this glorious region, and along the foot of these mountains, I have seen summer die as I never saw it die before. There has been a beauty and brightness and glory about the changing foliage this year, I never before witnessed. No drenching rains faded the colors before their time, and amid the clear weather and slight frosts, the summer has died like the dolphin, changing from beauty to beauty; and Autumn, the usually sober, serious, sober Autumn, has seemed the most frolicsome fellow of all the year. Stand in one of these deep valleys, and look around you on the shores and hill-slopes and mountain ridges! Autumn, with his brush and colors, has been painting with the most reckless prodigality and in endless variety of beauty and brightness. There is no end to his whims and conceits—the changed landscape seems the work of one in his most joyous, frolicsome mood. There stands a single maple tree; Autumn approached it last night, and apparently from a mere whim, threw his brush over the top, making it a scarlet red one third of the way down, while the other portion he left green as in its spring-time. He simply put a red cap on it and passed on. On another, he has run his brush along a single limb, which flashes out from the deep bosom of green in singular contrast. Yonder is an open grove which he has hurried through, touching here and there a tree with his reckless brush, till it is spotted up with all the colors of the rainbow. He has painted one all yellow, another all red, a third left untouched, and a fourth sprinkled over with a shower of colors, as if he had simply shaken his brush over it in mirth.

He has brought out colors where you never discovered anything but barrenness before. A yellow wreath is running along a rock and festooning a tree, where yesterday was only an humble unseen vine.

He has painted it in a single night. He has trod the gloomy swamp also, and lit up its solemn arcades with brightness and beauty. The bushes that lifted themselves modestly beside the dark fir trees, unnoticed before, he has touched with his pencil, while the evergreens, which he always avoids, stand in their native greenness—and lo, a yellow lake is spread under their sombre tops, as if a flood of molten gold had suddenly been poured through them. He has tipped the bush that dips the water with his pencil, and lo, the liquid mirror blushes with the reflection at morning. Like a giant he has stood at the base of the sky-seeking mountain, and swept his brush with a bold stroke all over its forest-covered sides, till it fairly dazzles the eye as the evening sunbeams flood it. There, where the ridges stoop into a long steady slope, he has wrought on a grander scale. The different nature of the soil has given birth to several varieties of timber, which lie like so many separate strata for miles along the mountain side; and here he has swept his brush in long stripes of yellow and red and green and gold, till acres on acres of carpeting spread away on the vision, while here and there separate clumps of trees have been touched with variegated hues to serve as figures in the magnificent ground work. It is astonishing how well Autumn understands the effect of light, especially as he works so much in the dark. But there, on the bold spur of that hill, right where the sunlight falls at evening through a gorge in the western range, he has laid on his richest and most gorgeous colors. And when the western sky is melting and flowing into fluid gold, and the glowing orb of day is swimming in its own splendor as it sinks to rest, it pours its full brightness upon that already bright projection, till it is converted into a throne of light.

Thus does this frolicsome Autumn roam abroad, with brush and colors in hand, obeying no law but that of beauty. But while he paints on such a grand scale, and with such long sweeps, and so rapidly, too, finishing millions of acres in a single night, he omits none of the details. Each leaf is as carefully shaded, and as delicately touched as if miniature painting was his only profession.

XXXII.

DIRECTIONS TO THE TRAVELER.

There are several routes to the region described in the foregoing letters. One goes by way of Lake George, where you take a wagon to Chester and Schroon Lake. From this point you can go either to Long Lake, or the Adirondack Iron Works.

Another is by way of Westport on Lake Champlain, where you take a wagon to Elizabethtown. At the latter place, as at Chester on the other route, you will obtain all the information necessary as to the best way of getting into the woods.

A third route goes by way of Keysville. Launching your boats on the Saranac River, you pass up it, carrying your boat around rapids—sailing through beautiful lakes, until at length you cross over to Raquette River up which you can wind your tedious way day after day until you reach Raquette Lake.

On the western side you start from Rome and go to Boonville, thence to Brown's tract, where you take boats for the Raquette, &c. There is another route still, leading in on the southern side from New Amsterdam, the particulars of which I am unacquainted with.

In passing through this region, one should never wander from his guide, for it does not require more than a mile's aberration sometimes to lose one effectually. Neither should he, even *with* his guide, depart far from the water courses, for it is almost impossible to get through the woods. The quantities of fallen timber scattered throughout the forest in every direction—huge trees lying across each other, presenting an endless succession of barricades and impenetrable thickets, arrest the traveler at every step. A direct line cannot be pursued, and a man might work hard all day and not make ten miles' progress. And more than this, away from the lakes and streams you are not sure of game, especially on the higher grounds. These mountains are silent as the grave—the owl perchance being the only bird you will see in a day's tramp. It is true, deer, bear, wolves, panthers, and moose roam over them, or retire to their summits to take the cool air and escape the flies of the lower grounds, but you make such a thrashing among the branches, both green and dry, that they are off, long before you come in sight of them. These forests are so dense that you can see but a short distance ahead. A good rifle, a knife, three or four shirts, and a blanket or overcoat, making a package of only a few pounds weight, must be all that you take with you—for, in the first place, your rifle weighs from eight to twelve pounds, and in the second place, you are often compelled to carry that of your guide also, together with a tin kettle, perhaps, or pan which you need in cooking. Over the portages he can carry only the boat, and it would be a great waste of time to compel him to go back after the traps. Your guide must have also a little sack of Indian meal with which to make Johnny-cakes. A small bit of pork is likewise desirable to fry your trout with. Thus equipped, with a good pair of legs under you, a spirit not easily discouraged, and a love for the wild, and free, you can have a glorious tramp—enjoy magnificent scenery—catch trout and kill deer to your heart's content, and come back to civilized life a healthier and a better man.

www.ingramcontent.com/pod-product-compliance
Lightning Source LLC
LaVergne TN
LVHW020230110826
845151LV00003B/876

* 9 7 8 1 4 2 5 5 3 0 5 2 5 *